THE FAITH
&
THE FURY

A Millennium of Religious Genocide

Malcolm Wruntte

GW00703187

Forever In Print Ltd London

Forever In Print

King Street, London W6

First published in Great Britain 2023

This Edition published 2023

INTRODUCTION

Religiosity has been with the Human race almost since the beginning of our species' existence, without known warfare resulting until just one thousand and thirty years ago, 1096, when a Roman Catholic pope in Rome requested that the lands, approximating a five hundred kilometre radius around Jerusalem, the birth place of Jesus Christ, were to be seized and put under Christian control. The Faith & the Fury charts that invasion and one millennium of religiously motivated conflicts that followed, resulting in the often-violent deaths of over sixteen million victims and combatants in that one thousand odd years.

CONTENTS

THE FIRST CRUSADE

An initial Crusade, carried out in the three year period from 1096 to 1099, was the first of a series of religious wars, instigated and supported by the Roman Catholic Church in the medieval period whose objective was the recovery of the lands, roughly corresponding to the modern State of Israel and the Palestinian territories, and remove them from Islamic control, since, by the eleventh century the Turk/Persian Seljuk Empire had taken over the region around Jerusalem which threatened both local Christian populations and the Roman Byzantine empire. Pope Urban II supported a Byzantine request for military assistance and also put out a strong demand for faithful Christians to undertake an armed pilgrimage to Jerusalem, which was met with widespread enthusiasm across Western Europe. Thousands strong mobs of mostly poor Christians led by Peter the Hermit, a French priest, were the first to respond. What has been called the People's Crusade passed through Germany and indulged in many anti-Jewish activities which included the "Rhineland massacres" of 1096, a mass slaughter of Jewish people.

In what later become known as the Princes' Crusade, titled European noblemen and their followers departed in August, 1096 and arrived at Constantinople between November and April the next year. In total, and including non-combatants, the forces are estimated to have numbered as many as one hundred thousand.

The crusader forces gradually arrived in Anatolia and in June an initial crusader victory was made before, in July, they won the Battle of Dorylaeum, tackling Turkish lightly armoured mounted archers. After a problematic march through Anatolia, the crusaders started the Siege of Antioch, capturing the city in June 1098. They got to Jerusalem in June 1099 and the siege there resulted in the city being taken during a one-month assault, during which its defenders were ruthlessly massacred. A Muslim counterattack was fought off later that year at the Battle of Ascalon, ending the First Crusade, after which most of the crusaders returned home.

THE RHINELAND MASSACRES

The Rhineland Massacres, additionally known as the German Crusade, were a series of mass murders of Jews perpetrated by mobs of French and German Christians of the People's Crusade in the year 1096. These massacres are sometimes seen as the first in a sequence of antisemitic events which culminated in the Nazi Holocaust of the 1930's and 1940's. Leaders of crusaders involved in these massacres included Peter the Hermit, a French priest.

The preaching of the First Crusade inspired outbreaks of anti-Jewish violence and in parts of France and Germany. Jewish people were perceived as equally an enemy as were Muslims and also held responsible for the crucifixion of Jesus Christ. Many French and Germans asked themselves why they would travel thousands of miles to fight non-believers in North Africa when there were already plenty of non-believers far closer to home.

It is moreover probable that the crusaders were motivated by their requirement for cash. Many of them had to get into debt in order to purchase weaponry and equipment for the expedition and since the Catholic Church forbade money lending for profit, many crusaders inevitably found themselves indebted to Jewish lenders. Later, having armed-up by taking on debt, the crusaders rationalized the killing of Jews as an extension of their Catholic mission. This was the first time there had been such an intense action against Jews by Catholics since the mass expulsions and forced conversions of the seventh century.

The angers that had been aroused within the Catholic community by Pope Urban II's call for the first crusade had propelled the persecution of Jews onto a new level in history on which previous constraints no longer had leverage. One prominent medieval author wrote that before "a war in behalf of the Lord" could be fought, it was essential that the Jews convert; those who resisted were "deprived of their goods, massacred, and expelled from the cities.

The first violence to break out happened in France when the officers, nobles and common people who took counsel together and plotted and construed a clear the way to go forward toward Jerusalem.

During the June and July of 1095, Jewish communities in the Rhineland were attacked after which some Jews dispersed eastward to escape the persecution.

Adding to the general Catholic suspicion of Jews at the time, when the raging hordes of French members of the People's Crusade got to the Rhine, they had run short of provisions. To replenish their supplies, they took to plundering Jewish food and property while also trying to force Jews to convert to Catholicism.

Not all of the crusaders who had run short of supplies resorted to homicide but others, such as Peter the Hermit, exercised extortion instead. Whilst there are no sources which appear to claim that Peter the Hermit preached against the Jews, he is said to have carried a letter with him from the Jews of France to the community at Trier which urged them to supply provisions to Peter and his army. Whatever Peter's own intentions towards the Jews was, there were men claiming to follow after him who felt free to massacre Jews as of their own free will and to rob them of their possessions.

In some cases Jewish residents survived after being forced into involuntary baptism, as happened in Germany at Regensburg, where a marauding mob rounded up the Jewish community and forced them into the Danube where they carried out a mass baptism. However, after the crusaders had exited the region, the Jews soon reverted to practicing Judaism. The crusade of the priest Folkmar, beginning in Saxony, persecuted Jews in Magdeburg and later, in Prague in Bohemia.

However, the Catholic Bishop Cosmas did try to prevent forced conversions and the entire Catholic hierarchy in Bohemia preached against such acts. But, in general, the crusader mobs did not fear retribution, since the local law enforcement had no jurisdiction to pursue them further than their current locality and also, lacked the ability to identify and prosecute individuals from the mob. The latent objections of the clergy were largely ignored because of this, and the mob tended to think that anyone preaching mercy to the Jews was doing so merely because they had given in to Jewish bribery.

In late June of that year, the crusader mob of Gottschalk was welcomed by King Coloman of Hungary before they soon took to plundering the countryside and causing alcohol-fuelled disorder. Coloman then demanded they disarm and once their weapons had been removed, the angry Hungarians jumped upon them and caused the whole plain to be coated with corpses and blood.

The largest of the crusades most involved in attacking Jews, was that led by Count Emicho of Flonheim who set off in the early summer of 1096 with an army of around ten thousand personnel. They proceeded through the Rhine valley, towards the Main River and then to the Danube.

The Holy Roman Emperor Henry IV ordered that the Jews be protected when he learned of Emicho's intentions. After some Jews were slaughtered at Metz, the Bishop of Speyer gave shelter to the Jewish inhabitants but even though, some Jews of Speyer were still slain by crusaders that May. At least eight hundred Jewish people were massacred in Worms when they refused Catholic baptism.

News of this crusade spread quickly, and Emicho was prevented from entering Mainz by Bishop Ruthard but he took an offering of gold raised by the Jews of Mainz in hope to gain his favor and their safety. Bishop Ruthard also tried to protect the Jews by hiding them in his lightly fortified palace. none-the-less, Emicho did not prevent his followers from entering the city on the 27th of May and a massacre was carried out.It was common amongst the business classes of Christians, in Mainz, to have working ties with Jews and to give them shelter from the mobs. These people joined with the militia of the bishop and the town's military governor, in fighting off the first waves of crusaders. This stand however, had to be discontinued as crusaders continued to arrive in ever greater numbers, and then the militia of the bishop together with the bishop himself fled and left the Jews behind who were then slaughtered by the crusaders. Many ordinary citizens in Mainz and other the towns were pulled along into the frenzy and joined in the persecution and pillaging.

Mainz was where the greatest violence took place with at least eleven hundred Jews being killed by troops operating under Clarambaud and Thomas.

Given the choice between running, death or conversion, some Jews opted in desperation for a fourth alternative: active martyrdom, which was the killing their family and themselves.

Emicho continued towards Hungary, but Coloman of Hungary refused to allow them through. Count Emicho and his army then besieged Moson. But the morale of the crusader mob began to fail, which encouraged the Hungarians, and most of Emicho's mob was slaughtered or drowned in the river.

THE SECOND CRUSADE

A crusade, lasting between 1145 and 1149, was the second major crusade launched from Europe. It was started in response to the fall of the County of Edessa in 1144 to the Atabeg of Zengi. Edessa had been founded during the First Crusade by King Baldwin the 1st. It had been the first Crusader state to be founded but it was also the first to fall.

The Second Crusade was announced by the Catholic Pope Eugene III and was the first of the crusades to be led by European kings, particularly Louis VII of France and Conrad III of Germany, with support from a number of other European noblemen. The armies of the kings marched across Europe and, after crossing Byzantine territory into Anatolia, they were both defeated by the Seljuk Turks.

Louis and Conrad and the survivors of their armies reached Jerusalem and participated in 1148 in an attack on Damascus, which ended in their retreat. In the conclusion, the crusade in the east was a failure for the crusaders and a victory for the Muslims and ultimately had a key influence on the fall of Jerusalem and give rise to the Third Crusade at the end of the 12th century.

THE THIRD CRUSADE

The Third Crusade, which was carried out from 1189 until 1192, was an attempt to reconquer the Holy Land following the capture of Jerusalem by the Ayyubid sultan Saladin in 1187. It was spearheaded by three European monarchs of Western Christianity; these being, Philip II of France, Richard I of England and Frederick I, a Holy Roman Emperor and is also known as the "Kings' Crusade". It was in-part successful, recapturing the strategic cities of Acre and Jaffa and reversing most of Saladin's conquests. However, it failed to recapture Jerusalem, which was the main aim of the Crusade with its religious objectives.

After the failure of the Second Crusade the sultan, Saladin, brought both the Egyptian and Syrian forces under his leadership and used them to reduce the Crusader states and to recapture Jerusalem in 1187. Inflated then with religious zeal, King Henry II of England and King Philip II of France ended their conflict with each other in order to join and lead a new crusade. However, the death of King Henry in 1189 resulted in the English contingent came under the command of his successor, King Richard I of England. The sixty-seven year old German Emperor Frederick Barbarossa likewise responded to the call to arms and lead a large army across the Balkans and Anatolia. Frederick achieved some victories against the Seljuk Sultanate of Rûm, but he died whilst crossing a river in June 1190 before reaching the Holy Land, his death causing widespread grief among the German Crusaders causing most of his troops to return home.

After the Crusaders had driven the Ayyubid army from the city of Acre, French king Philip left the Holy Land in August 1191 and following a major victory by the Crusaders at the Battle of Arsuf, most of the coastline of the Levant was returned to Christian control.

On the 2nd of September 1192, English king Richard 1 and the sultan Saladin finalized the Treaty of Jaffa, which recognised Muslim control over Jerusalem but allowed unarmed Christian pilgrims and merchants to visit the city.

King Baldwin the fourth of Jerusalem died in 1185 which left the Kingdom of Jerusalem to his nephew Baldwin the fifth but the following year, Baldwin the fifth died and his mother Princess Sybilla, sister of Baldwin IV, crowned herself queen and her husband, Guy, king. Raynald of Châtillon, who had backed Sybilla's claim to the throne, raided a wealthy cara-

van travelling from Egypt to Syria, and had its con-
stituents thrown in prison which broke the truce
between the Kingdom of Jerusalem and Saladin. Saladin demanded the freedom of the prisoners and
release of their cargo. The freshly crowned King Guy
requested that Raynald give in to Saladin's demands.
However, Raynald refused to follow the king's
instruction.

This outrageous decision by Raynald gave the sultan Saladin the excuse he needed to take the offensive
against the Kingdom of Jerusalem but in 1187 he laid
siege to the city of Tiberias. King Guy, after seeking
advice from Raynald, marched his army to the Horns
of Hattin outside of Tiberias where Saladin's forces
fought the Frankish army and destroyed it in the ensuing Battle of Hattin in July 1187.

Saladin beheaded Raynald for past betrayals but
honoured tradition with King Guy, sending him to
Damascus and eventually allowing him to be ran-
somed by his people.

By the end of 1187 Saladin had re-taken both Acre
and Jerusalem. Upon hearing the news, Pope Urban III
is said to have collapsed and died during October 1187.

The next pope, Gregory VIII, called for a new crusade to the Holy Land. The crusade of the Holy Roman
Emperor, the sixty-six years old Frederick Barbarossa,
was more meticulously planned and organized than its
predecessors.

Near the end of October 1187, three weeks after Saladin's capture of Jerusalem, Pope Gregory VIII wrote to the German episcopate announcing his election and ordered them to win the German nobility over to a new crusade. The next month Frederick received letters that had been sent to him from the rulers of the Crusader states in the East requesting him to rush to their aid.

After making Crusader vows, Frederick announced a general expedition against the pagans and, in doing so, complied with the Pope's instructions. He instructed the period for preparation to be between the 17th of April 1188 and the 8th of April 1189 and planned that the army were to assemble at Regensburg on Saint George's Day, the 23rd of April 1189. To avoid the crusade degenerating into an undisciplined rabble, participants were told they must have at least three marks with them, enough money to support a man for two years.

At Strasbourg, Frederick laid a special small tax on the Jewish residents of Germany to fund the crusade but he also put the them under his protection and forbade anyone to carry out antisemitic preaching. Whilst the First and Second Crusades in Germany had been tarred with violence against Jewish people, the Third Crusade spurred on an outbreak of violence against Jews in England.

Because Frederick had signed a treaty of agreement with Saladin in 1175, he felt it necessary to give Saladin notice of the termination of their alliance and he sent Count Henry II of Dietz to present an ultimatum to Saladin. The sultan was asked to withdraw from the lands he had conquered, to return the True Cross to the Church of the Holy Sepulchre and to make reparation for the Christians who had been killed in his conquests.

Some days after Christmas in 1188, Frederick received Hungarian, Byzantine, Serbian, Seljuk and Ayyubid envoys in Nuremberg where the Hungarians and Seljuks promised provisions and safe-conduct for the crusaders. The envoy for Serbia announced that their prince would receive Frederick in Niš and an agreement was reached with the Byzantine envoy.

Frederick was the first of the three kings to set out for the Holy Land and on the 15th of April 1189 in Haguenau, he formally and symbolically accepted the staff and scrip of a pilgrim. He arrived in Regensburg between the 7th and the 11th of May where the army had begun to gather on the 1st of May. Frederick, however, was disappointed by the size of the force awaiting him, but was dissuaded from calling off the attack plan when he found out that an international force had already advanced to the Hungarian border.

Frederick set out with an army of up to twenty thousand men, including two thousand knights. After leaving Germany, Frederick's army was increased by the addition of an assemblage of two thousand men led by the Hungarian prince Géza.

Frederick sailed from Regensburg during the May of 1189, but most of the army had left earlier by land for the Hungarian border. On the 16th of May, he ordered that the village of Mauthausen be burned because it had levied a toll on the army. He celebrated Pentecost, encamped across from Hungarian Pressburg.

From Pressburg, the Hungarian envoys escorted the crusaders to Esztergom, where the King of Hungary greeted them and provided boats, wine, bread and barley to the army. Frederick stayed in Esztergom for four days after which the king of Hungary accompanied the army to the Byzantine border at Belgrade.

The army, still accompanied by Béla III, departed from Belgrade at the beginning of July, crossed the Morava river and headed for Braničevo, which was the seat of the local Byzantine administration since Belgrade had been damaged in recent wars with the Hungarians and Serbs.

At Braničevo, Béla III said his goodbyes and returned to Hungary, but, first he gave the crusaders wagons and in return Frederick gave him his boats after realizing they'd no longer be travelling up the river.

The Burgundian assemblage under Archbishop

Aimo II of Tarentaise and another from Metz caught up with the army at Braničcvo where the duke of Braničevo provided the army with provisions to last eight days. The bolstered army which included a Hungarian contingent, left Braničevo in mid July following the ancient road, the Via Militaris, that led to Constantinople.

Frederick was welcomed by Stefan Nemanja in Niš with pomp on the 27th of July. Although the Serbian ruler asked the emperor to invest him with his domains, Frederick refused on the grounds that he was on a pilgrimage and did not wish to harm Isaac.

Before leaving Niš, Frederick had Godfrey of Würzburg preach a sermon stressing the importance of discipline and the maintaining of the peace. He also made a reorganization of his army by dividing it into four, since it would be entering territory more firmly under Byzantine control and therefore less friendly.

The Swabian and Bavarian vanguard was commanded by the Duke of Swabia aided by Herman IV of Baden and Berthold III of Vohburg. The second division was made up of the Hungarian and Bohemian assemblages with their standard-bearers. The third was under commanded by the Duke of Merania aided by Bishop Diepold of Passau and the fourth, under Frederick's personal command.

The crusaders departed from Niš at the end of

July and got to Sofia on the 13th of August where they discovered the city virtually abandoned. The following day the crusaders quit Sofia and the forces under Peter of Brixey caught up with the leading army which arrived at Pazardzhik on the 20th of August, finding plenty of supplies. On the 24th of August, the imperial army got to Philippopolis finding that the Byzantine forces in the area had fled at their approach. The next day, Lectoforus' report was confirmed; that Hermann of Münster, Rupert of Nassau, Henry of Dietz and Markward von Neuenburg had been stripped of their possessions and openly mocked in presence of the Ayyubid ambassador. Later that day, James of Pisa, a Byzantine envoy, arrived with a letter from Isaac, referring to Frederick as "king of Germany" and refusing him the imperial title. Moreover, it accused him of plotting to put his son Frederick on the throne of Constantinople. He nevertheless offered to follow the agreement of December 1188 to transport the crusaders across the River Dardanelles if he received hostages, including Duke Frederick and six bishops, plus envoys he had put under arrest. After that the crusaders resorted to plunder and destroy tactics. A few days later in August, the crusaders seized Philippopolis with its bountiful supplies.

Frederick attempted to contact the closest Byzantine commander, the protostrator Manuel Kamytzes and, getting no response, he attacked his army. Soon after, Duke Frederick and Duke Berthold occupied Berrhoë unopposed. Henry of Kalden occupied a castle named Scribention, and Bishop Diepold with Duke Berthold seized a further two towns and ten castles. At that time the local Armenian and Bulgarian residents swore oaths to Frederick to maintain supplies in Philippopolis for as long as the crusaders stayed. They held on there and in partial occupation of Macedonia until early November.

Emperor Isaac ordered Kamytzes to shadow the crusaders and trouble their hunting parties. Around the 22nd of November 1189, with about two thousand horsemen, Kamytzes arranged an ambush for the crusaders' supply caravan near Philippopolis. The crusaders got to know of this through the Armenian inhabitants of the fortress of Prousenos, where Kamytzes had his main camp. They then set off with five thousand cavalries to attack the Byzantine grouping. The two forces met unplanned close to Prousenos, and in the subsequent battle, Kamytzes was defeated.

After reaching Anatolia, Frederick was guaranteed safe passage through the province by the Turkish Sultanate of Rum, but instead suffered frequent Turkish hit-and-run attacks on his army. However, a Turkish army of ten thousand men was defeated at the Battle of Philomelion by only two thousand Crusaders which resulted in almost five thousand Turks being slain.

When Turkish raids against the Crusader army continued, Frederick made the decision to replenish his stock of animals and foodstuffs by taking over the Turkish capital of Iconium. On the 18th of May 1190, the German's defeated their Turkish enemies at the Battle of Iconium, plundering the city and slaughtering three thousand Turkish troops.

As he was crossing the Saleph River on the 10th of June 1190, Emperor Frederick's horse slipped which threw him against rocks after which he then drowned in the waters. Following this, much of his army returned to Germany by sea.

The emperor's son led the remaining five thousand men to Antioch where the Emperor's body was boiled to remove the flesh, then was interred in the Church of Saint Peter and his bones were bagged up to continue the crusade. Young Frederick requested the assistance of his kinsman Conrad of Montferrat to lead him safely to Acre where his father's bones were then buried. The imperial army failed to achieve its objective of capturing Jerusalem but it did capture the capital of the Seljuk Sultanate and wreaked major damage on Turkish forces with nearly ten thousand Turkish soldiers killed in the battles and skirmishes.

In England the first of two fleets departed during the solemn Christian religious observance of Lent.

After mooring in Lisbon, the fleet invaded Alvor and slaughtered its defenders before arriving in Acre at the start of September.

Leaving later, the De itinere navali fleet, was composed mainly of commoners and departed from Germany with eleven ships, but these were added to, after it arrived in Lisbon in early July, by an English fleet that had sailed two months earlier. It was then recruited by King Sancho I of Portugal to assist in an attack on the municipality of Silves. At the subsequent siege of Silves, the fleet had thirty-eight ships, including two from Brittany and Galicia and the city surrendered after forty-five days. The next fleet arrived at Acre between April and June 1190. There, wood and sail from its cogs was utilized to construct a field hospital, which eventually became known as the Teutonic Order.

During the summer of 1190, a single English ship separated from its fleet sailing into Silves while the city was being besieged by the Almohad Berbers and on the request of the former expeditioner, Bishop Nicholas, the English crusaders participated in the successful defence.

In January 1188, Henry II of England and Philip II of France ended their war with each other and then they both accepted the cross. Moreover, they both imposed a "Saladin tithe" on their citizens to help finance the enterprise. In Britain, Baldwin, the Archbishop of Canterbury, made an excursion through Wales and convinced three thousand men-at-arms there to decide to take up the cross.

After King Henry II of England died in July 1189, Richard 1 succeeded him and lost no time in commencing to raise funds for the crusade. In April 1190, King Richard's fleet lifted anchors from Dartmouth under the charge of Richard de Camville and Robert de Sablé, both on their way to meet their king in Marseille. Sections of this fleet assisted the Portuguese to defeat an Almohad counterattack against Santarém and Torres Novas. Richard and Philip II joined up in France at Vézelay and together set out on the 4th of July 1190, going as far as Lyon before they parted after agreeing to meet in Sicily. Richard with his entourage of about eight hundred, marched to Marseille where he found that his fleet had not arrived. Quickly tiring of waiting for them, he hired ships and left for Sicily on the 7th of August. He visited several places of interest in Italy en route and arrived in Messina on the 23rd of September. The English fleet eventually had arrived in Marseille on the 22nd of August, and finding that Richard had gone, sailed directly to Messina, and arrived before him in mid-September. Philip had procured a Genoese fleet to transport his army, which consisted of six hundred and fifty knights, thirteen hundred horses, and thirteen hundred squires to the Holy Land, via Sicily.

King Richard and his forces captured the city of city of Messina in Sicily on the 4th of October 1190. King Philip left Sicily directly for the Middle East on the 30th of March 1191 and arrived in Tyre that April. He joined the siege of Acre on the 20th of April. Shortly after setting sail from Sicily, King Richard's navy of over two hundred ships was impeded by a treacherous storm. Several ships ran aground, including one holding a large amount of treasure that had been amassed for the crusade and it was soon detected that Isaac Dukas Comnenus of Cyprus had taken away the treasure.

King Richard went into Limassol on the island of Cyprus on the 6th of May and met with Isaac, who agreed to return King Richard's treasures and to send five hundred of his fighting men to the Holy Land. King Richard made camp at Limassol, where he received a visit from Guy of Lusignan. However, once back at his fortress of Famagusta, Isaac broke his promise of hospitality and began trying to get Richard to leave Cyprus. Isaac's stance prompted Richard to take over the island, but he left some days before June.

The sultan Saladin let King Guy out of prison in 1189 and Guy then attempted to take command of the Christian forces at Tyre. However, Conrad of Montferrat had the power there after his successful defence of the city from Islamic attacks. Guy then turned his sights on the wealthy port of Acre, and he regrouped an army to besiege the city, also receiving aid from King Philip's freshly arrived French forces. The combined Christian forces however were not enough to repulse Saladin whose forces managed to besiege the Crusaders.

In the summer of 1190 Queen Sibylla died in one of many outbreaks of disease in their camp. King Guy, being king by right of marriage, attempted to keep his crown, even though the rightful heir was Sibylla's half-sister Isabella. Then, after a quickly arranged divorce from her husband, Humphrey IV of Toron, Isabella got married to Conrad of Montferrat and thereafter he claimed the kingship in her name.

During 1190 and 1191 the crusaders saw more occurrences of dysentery and fever, which resulted in the deaths of Frederick of Swabia, Patriarch Heraclius of Jerusalem, and Theobald V of Blois. During the Spring of 1191, King Leopold V of Austria arrived and assumed command of what was left of the imperial forces. King Philip of France arrived with his troops from Sicily in that May and a neighbouring army under Leo II of Cilician Armenia additionally arrived.

English King Richard arrived at the city of Acre on the 8th of June 1191 and instantly began directing the construction of siege weapons to attack the city, which was seized on the 12th of July. However, the three kings, Richard, Philip, and Leopold, quarrelled over the spoils of the victory. King Richard cast down the German standard from the city, insulting Leopold. In the resulting struggle for the kingship of Jerusalem, Richard supported Guy, while Philip and Leopold supported Conrad, a relation of them both. It was agreed that Guy would continue ruling but that Conrad would receive the crown upon Guy's death. Frustrated with Richard,Philip and Leopold took their armies and left the Holy Land that August after leaving seven thousand French crusaders and also five thousand silver marks to pay them.

It was on the 18th of June 1191, and shortly after King Richard's arrival at Acre, that he sent a messenger to Saladin asking for a face to face meeting. Saladin turned this down, declaring that it was normal only for kings to meet each other only after a peace treaty had been agreed, and after that it was not appropriate for them to make war upon each other. The king and the sultan therefore never met, although they did exchange some gifts and the king had a number of meetings with Al-Adil, Saladin's brother. Saladin wanted to negotiate with the king for the release of a captured Muslim warrior garrison, which included their women and children.

However, on that 20th of August, Richard decided the sultan had procrastinated too much and had twenty- seven hundred of the Muslim prisoners beheaded in full view of Saladin's army, which attempted unsuccessfully to rescue them. Saladin countered by having killed all of the Christian prisoners he had captured.

After the seizing of Acre, King Richard decided to march to the city of Jaffa since control of Jaffa was needed before an attack on Jerusalem could be attempted. However, on the 7th of September 1191, Saladin's forces attacked Richard's army at Arsuf, thirty miles north of Jaffa. Saladin attempted to cause Richard's army to break its but the king conserved his army's defensive formation. Richard then ordered a general counterattack, which won the battle and made Arsuf a valuable victory.

The Muslim forces were not destroyed, however, despite losing seven thousand men, but it did beat back which boosted the morale of the Crusaders. Moreover, Arsuf had dented Saladin's reputation as an invincible warrior and also proved Richard's courage as soldier and his skill as a commander. Richard was then able to sieze, defend, and hold on to Jaffa, a strategically important action towards securing Jerusalem.

After Richard took Jaffa, he established his new headquarters there and offered to restart negotiations with Saladin, The sultan, however, sent his brother, Al-Adil, to meet with Richard.

During November 1191 the Crusaders advanced inland towards Jerusalem and on the 12th of December, Saladin was pressured by his commanders to disband the greater part of his army. Realizing this, Richard pressed his army forward, and spent Christmas at the strategic hilltop of Latrun.

The army then marched to Beit Nuba which was just twelve miles from Jerusalem where Muslim morale was low and bad weather combined with fear of the Crusader army led to the decision to retreat back to the coast.

King Richard then requested that Conrad join him on campaign, but Conrad refused, excusing himself because of Richard's alliance with King Guy. Conrad too had been negotiating with Saladin as a security against any attempt by Richard to wrest Tyre from him for Guy. That April, however, Richard was forced to accept Conrad as king of Jerusalem after an election by the nobles of the kingdom. Before he could be crowned, Conrad was stabbed to death by two Assassins in the streets of Tyre. Eight days later, Richard's nephew, Henry II of Champagne, married Queen Isabella, who was pregnant with Conrad's child.

During the winter months of 1191, Richard's men occupied and refortified Ascalon, whose fortifications had earlier been burnt down by Saladin's men. In the Spring of 1192, there were continued negotiations and further skirmishing between the opposing forces. On the 22nd of May the strategically important fortified town of Darum on the frontiers of Egypt was taken by the crusaders, following five days of aggressive fighting. The Crusaders made further advances towards Jerusalem, and in June it came within sight of the city before being forced into retreat again.

The leader of the French contingent, the Duke of Burgundy, however, insisted that a direct attack on Jerusalem should be made. Richard said that he would join any attack on Jerusalem but only as a basic soldier and refused to lead the army. Left without a united command the army had little choice but to retreat back to the coast.

In July 1192, the armies of sultan Saladin, thousands strong, unexpectedly attacked and captured Jaffa.

Richard had been intending to return to England when he found out that Saladin and his men had captured Jaffa. Richard and a minimal force of few more than two thousand men sailed to Jaffa in a surprise sea attack. Richard's forces stormed Jaffa from their ships and the Ayyubids, who had been unprepared for a waterborne attack, were chased out from the city. Saladin's army, however, with numerical superiority, counter-attacked. Saladin intended a covert surprise attack at dawn but his forces were noticed. However, he carried on with the attack. His his men being lightly armoured were reduced by seven hundred killed by the arrows of the large numbers of Crusader crossbowmen. This battle to retake Jaffa ended in absolute failure for Saladin, who was forced to retreat which greatly strengthened the position of the coastal Crusader states.

In early September 1192, following Saladin's defeat at Jaffa, he was persuaded to finalize a treaty with Richard provisioning that Jerusalem would be under Muslim control, whilst allowing non-armed Christian pilgrims and traders to visit the city. Richard departed the Holy Land during the following month.

THE FOURTH CRUSADE

The Fourth Crusade was carried out from 1202 until 1204 AD. It was a Christian armed expedition called for in Rome by Pope Innocent III. The proposed objective of the missions was to recover the city of Jerusalem from Muslim-control, initially by defeating the Egyptian Ayyubid Sultanate which was the most powerful Muslim state at that time. However, a succession of monetary and diplomatic events led to both the Crusader army's 1202 siege of Zara and the sack of the Turkish city of Constantinople in 1204. Constantinople was the capital of the Greek Christian-controlled Byzantine Empire. This resulted in the partitioning of the Byzantine Empire by the Crusaders.

The Republic of Venice in Italy made a contract with the Crusader to build a fleet of boats to carry their invasion personnel. However, the Crusader's leaders overestimated by far the number of fighters who would embark from Venice, largely because many sailed from alternative ports and the men who turned up to sail were unable to pay the agreed price. In lieu of payment, the Venetian Doge asked the Crusaders to support him in attacking the rebellious city of Zadar on the eastern Adriatic coast and this, November 1202, led to the siege and sack of Zara and it was the first attack against a Catholic city by a Catholic Crusader army, after which, the city was brought under Venetian control. When the Pope discovered this, he temporarily excommunicated the Crusader army.

In early 1203, on the way to Jerusalem, the Crusader leadership made an agreement with the Byzantine Alexios Angelos to divert their main force to Constantinople for the purpose of restoring his overthrown father, Isaac, as emperor and Isaac would then add his support to their invasion of Jerusalem. In June 1203 the main Crusader army reached Constantinople, while the majority of crusaders, continued to the city of Acre.

In August 1203, after the siege of Constantinople, Alexios was crowned co-emperor, but, in January 1204 he was deposed by a popular uprising, thus depriving the Crusaders of their expected bounty payments. Following the murder of Alexios during the following month, the Crusaders decided on the outright conquest of Constantinople and during April 1204, they captured and raided the city's vast wealth and very few of the Crusaders continued onwards to the Holy Land.

The Crusader conquest of Constantinople resulted

in the splitting of the Byzantine Empire into three states, focused around Nicaea, Trebizond and Epirus. The Crusaders then founded several new Crusader states whose presence almost immediately led to war with the Byzantine successor states and with the Bulgarian Empire. Constantinople was however recovered and restored the Byzantine Empire in 1261.

The Fourth Crusade was thought by many to have laid foundations to an East–West Schism since that crusade greatly weakened the Byzantine-Roman Empire and contributed to its decline and fall.

During the eleven years between 1176 and 1187, the sultan Saladin conquered most of the Crusader holdings in the Eastern Mediterranean region. The Crusader states were then reduced by Saladin to little more than three cities along the coast of the Mediterranean Sea, these being, Tyre, Tripoli and Antioch.

In September 1192, the Treaty of Jaffa was signed with Saladin, bringing the crusade to an end, a truce which would last for forty-four months. The crusade also marked a considerable escalation in longstanding unease between the feudal states of western Europe and the Byzantine Empire.

The sultan, Saladin died on the 4th of March 1193, before the expiration of the truce with the Crusaders. His empire was disputed over and split up between three of his sons and two of his brothers.

The Kingdom of Jerusalem was at that time ruled

by Henry II of Champagne who signed an extension of the truce with the Egyptian sultan, al-Aziz Uthman. However, in 1197, the peace was disrupted by the arrival of the German Crusade of that year. Without the permission of Henry of Champagne, the Germans assaulted the territory of al-Adil I of Damascus, who countered them by attacking Jaffa. The unexpected death of Henry II of Champagne prevented an adequate protection of the port and the city was forcibly taken. The Germans, however, did succeed in capturing Beirut in the northern territories.

Henry II of Champagne was succeeded by Aimery of Cyprus, who signed a truce with al-Adil of sixty-eight months on the 1st of July 1198 which preserved the status quo. Jaffa remained in Muslim hands, but its battered fortifications were unable to be rebuilt.

Before the expiry date of the new truce which was the 1st of March 1204, the governor, al-Adil, succeeded in uniting the former empire of Saladin, thus acquiring Egypt in 1200 and Aleppo two years after which meant that his provinces almost totally surrounded the size-reduced Crusader states.

The city of Constantinople had been in existence for eight hundred and seventy four years at the time of the Fourth Crusade and was the largest and most cultured Christian city that existed. At its height, the city was home to an estimated population of approximately half a million people defended by thirteen miles of triple walls. Constantinople's location made it not only the capital of the surviving Eastern Roman Empire but also a mercantile centre that dominated trade routes from the Mediterranean to the Black Sea, China, India and Persia/Iran. Because of this, it was a rival and also a appealing target for the aggressive new states of the west, particularly the Republic of Venice.

In 1195, the Byzantine Emperor Isaac II was overthrown in a palace coup. Ascending as Alexios III, the new emperor had his brother blinded and exiled. Inadequate on the battlefield, Isaac had also shown he was not a competent ruler who had allowed the treasury to dwindle and his actions in wastefully distributing military weapons and supplies as gifts to his supporters had weakened the empire's defences. The new emperor was to prove himself little better. Eager to strengthen his position, he bankrupted the treasury and his attempts to secure the support of semi-autonomous border commanders diluted central authority.

Pope Innocent III succeeded to the papacy in January 1198, and the calling for a new crusade became a primary goal of his pontificate. His call was mostly ignored by the European monarchs since the Germans were resisting against Papal power and England and France were still warring against each other. However, partly due to the preaching of Fulk of

Neuilly, a crusading army was finally brought together at a tournament in 1199. The elected leader died in 1201 and was replaced by Boniface of Montferrat.

Earlier crusades had focused on Palestine and had involved the slow movement of large and disorganised armies across a generally hostile Anatolia. Egypt was now the foremost Muslim power in the eastern Mediterranean but also an important trading partner of Venice. An attack on Egypt would need to be a maritime operation and would require the creation of a fleet. In March 1201 negotiations were opened with Venice, which agreed to transport thirty-three and a half thousand crusaders. This project required a full year of preparation for the Venetians to build numerous ships and to train the sailors who would man them. The crusader army was expected to consist of four and a half thousand knights together with four and a half thousand horses, nine thousand squires, and twenty thousand foot-soldiers.

Most of the crusading forces that set out from Venice in early October 1202 having originated from areas within France and including men from Blois, Champagne, Amiens, Saint-Pol, the Île-de-France, and Burgundy. Several other regions of Europe sent substantial legions as well, including Flanders and Montferrat. Other important groupings came from the Holy Roman Empire, including men under the

abbot of Paris Abbey and Bishop Conrad of Halber-
stadt, together in alliance with the Venetian forces led
by the doge, Enrico Dandolo. The crusade was
planned to be ready to sail by the end of June, 1203
and head directly for the city of Cairo, an agreement
ratified by Pope Innocent, but including a weighty
ban on attacking any Christian states.

There was no absolute agreement among the crusaders that they should all sail from Venice and many
chose to sail from Flanders, Marseille, or Genoa.
However, by May 1202, the greater part of the crusader army had been collected from Venice and the
Venetians had kept to their part of the agreement.
There awaited fifty war galleys and four hundred and
fifty transports which was enough for triple the
assembled army. The Venetians, under their aged
and blind Doge, would not allow the crusaders leave
without paying the full amount agreed to which was
eighty-five thousand silver marks. The crusaders
could only initially pay thirty-five thousand silver
marks and the Doge threatened to keep them
interned unless full payment was made so a further
fourteen thousand marks were collected, reducing
the crusaders to extreme poverty. This was a catastrophe for the Venetians, who had stopped their
commerce for a of time in order to prepare this
expedition. In addition, about fourteen thousand
men were needed to man the fleet, putting further

pressures on the Venetian economy.

Doge Dandolo and other Venetians considered what to do about the crusade. It was not big enough to pay its fee, but disbanding the force gathered would wound Venetian prestige and lead to substantial financial and trading loss. Dandolo, who joined the crusade during a public ceremony in the church of San Marco di Venezia, suggested that the crusaders pay their debts by badgering ports and towns down the Adriatic to collect funds. This plan culminated in an attack on the port of Zara in Dalmatia. The city had been dominated economically by Venice throughout the twelfth century but had rebelled in 1181, allying itself with King Emeric of Hungary and Croatia. Subsequent Venetian attempts to recover control of Zara had been repulsed, and by 1202 the city was economically independent and under the protection of the King.

King Emeric was Catholic and had himself taken the cross in the period 1195/96. Many of the crusaders were against attacking Zara, and some refused to participate altogether and returned home or travelled to the Holy Land on their own.

In 1202, Pope Innocent III, despite wanting to secure papal authority over Byzantium, forbade the crusaders of Western Christendom from committing atrocities against their Christian neighbours. However, his instruction, delivered by Peter of Lucedio, did not reach the army in time, whose bulk arrived at Zara on the 10th and the 11th of November 1202 and the attack proceeded. The inhabitants of Zara brought attention to the fact that they were fellow Catholics by hanging banners marked with crosses from their windows and the walls of the city. Nevertheless, the city fell on the 24th of November 1202 after a brief siege and there followed extensive pillaging after which the Venetians and other crusaders came to blows over the division of the spoils. Order was regained and the leaders of the expedition agreed to spend Winter in Zara, while considering their next move.

When the Pope heard of the sacking of Zara, he wrote to the crusaders, excommunicating them and ordering them to Jerusalem. When the Crusaders arrived at Constantinople in June 1203, the city had a population of approximately half a million people with a garrison of fifteen thousand men and a fleet of twenty galleys.

The main objective of the crusaders was to put Alexios IV on the Byzantine throne so that they could receive the large payments he had promised them. First the crusaders attacked and were repulsed from Chalcedon and Chrysopolis, suburbs of the larger city. Here, they won a cavalry skirmish in which they defeated five hundred Byzantines with just eighty Frankish knights.

To take the whole city, the crusaders first needed to cross the Bosphorus strait and around two hundred ships, horse transports, and galleys floated the crusading army across the water, where Alexios III had the Byzantine army in battle formation along the shore. The Crusader knights charged directly out of the horse transports causing the Byzantine army to flee south. The Crusaders followed and attacked the Tower of Galata which held a garrison of mercenary troops of English, Danish, and Italian origin.

As the crusaders laid siege to the Tower of Galata, the defenders consistently suffered bloody losses. The tower was rapidly taken as a result and the Golden Horn waterway now lay open to the Crusaders, and the Venetian fleet entered. The Crusaders sailed near to Constantinople with ten galleys to display the would-be new king. However, from the city walls, the citizens taunted the puzzled crusaders who thought that they would rise up to welcome Alexios as a liberator.

On the 11th of July, the Crusaders took positions near the Palace of Blachernae but their first attacks were repulsed. On the 17th of July four divisions attacked the land walls while the Venetian fleet attacked the sea walls from the sea. The Venetians took a wall section of twenty-five towers but the Varangian guard held off the Crusaders from the land wall. A resulting fire destroyed one hundred and twenty acres of the city and left about twenty thousand people homeless.

In January 1204, the blinded and disabled Isaac II died, after, in proceeding months, opposition to his son and co-emperor Alexios IV had grown. A nobleman named Alexios Doukas became the leader of the anti-crusader faction within the Byzantine leadership. He was well-placed to move against the increasingly isolated Alexios IV, whom he overthrew, imprisoned, and had strangled that February. Doukas was then crowned as Emperor Alexios V and he immediately moved to have the city fortifications strengthened and ordered additional forces to the city.

The Venetians and crusaders were angered by the murder of their supposed patron and demanded that Mourtzouphlos honour the contract that Alexios had promised. When the Byzantine emperor refused, the Crusaders besieged the city once again but bad weather conditions were a serious hindrance to them.

On the 12th of April 1204, the weather conditions finally favoured the crusaders and they sacked Constantinople for three days, during which many ancient and medieval Greco-Roman works of art were stolen or ruined. Many of the non-combatant population of the city were killed and their property looted. Despite the threat of excommunication, the crusaders destroyed, defiled and looted the city's churches and monasteries of about nine hundred thousand silver marks. The Venetians received one hundred and fifty thousand silver marks that were their due, while the crusaders received fifty thousand silver marks. A further one hundred thousand silver marks were divided evenly up between the crusaders and Venetians.

Constantinople had become an virtual museum of ancient and Byzantine art. The Crusaders vented their contempt for the Greeks most dramatically in the desecration of the greatest Church in Christendom when they smashed the silver iconostasis, the icons and the holy books of Hagia Sophia, and seated upon the patriarchal throne a whore who sang coarse songs as they drank wine from the Church's holy vessels. The division of East and West, which had ensued over the centuries, culminated in the heinous massacres that accompanied the conquest of Constantinople.

The defeat of Byzantium, which was already in a state of decline, accelerated the degeneration that resulted in the Byzantines becoming easy victims of the Turks. The Fourth Crusade and the crusading movement generally thus resulted, ultimately, in a victory for Islam, a reversal of its original purpose.

THE ALBIGENSIAN CRUSADE

The Albigensian Crusade which lasted from 1209 until 1229 was a military and ideological campaign begun by Pope Innocent III to eradicate Catharism in the French province of Languedoc.It resulted in the significant reduction of practicing Cathars and a realignment of the County of Toulouse with the French crown.

The Cathars originated from a reform movement in the Balkan Bogomil churches of requesting what they saw as a return to the Christian direction of perfection, poverty and preaching. The reforms were a reaction against the often perceived scandalous and dissolute lifestyles of the Catholic clergy in southern France.

Between 1022 and 1163, the Cathars were condemned by church councils, the last of which, held at Tours, declared that they should be put into prison and have their property confiscated. However, Innocent III's diplomatic attempts to turn back Catharism were met with little success and he then declared a crusade against the Cathars. He offered the lands of the Cathar heretics to any French nobleman willing to take up arms.

In the six years from 1209 to 1215, the Crusaders were greatly successful. They captured Cathar lands and methodically deminished the movement. But from 1215 to 1225, a series of revolts brought many of the lands into renewed crusade resulted in the recapturing of these territories and the driving of Catharism underground.

THE FIFTH CRUSADE

The Fifth Crusade, which was carried out from 1217 until 1221 AD, was a campaign in a sequence of Crusades spearheaded by Western Europeans. It was in order to re-acquire Jerusalem and the remainder of the Holy Land through initially conquering Egypt. Egypt was at that time ruled by a powerful Ayyubid sultanate, headed by al-Adil, the brother of Saladin.

After the failure of the Fourth Crusade, Innocent III had again began calling for a further crusade, and commenced organizing Crusading armies led by Andrew II of Hungary and Leopold VI of Austria. An initial campaign in late 1217 in Syria was inconclusive, and Andrew II of Hungary departed. A German army led by cleric Oliver of Paderborn, and a mixed army of Dutch, Flemish and Frisian soldiers led by William I of Holland eventually joined the Crusade in Acre. There, cardinal Pelagius Galvani arrived as papal legate and de facto leader of the Crusade and was supported by John of Brienne and the Templars, Hospitallers and Teutonic Knights.

Following a successful siege of Damietta in 1219, the Crusaders occupied the port for two years. Al-Kamil, by then sultan of Egypt, offered tempting peace terms which included the return of Jerusalem to Christian rule. The sultan was refused by Pelagius more than once and the Crusaders marched south towards Cairo in July 1221. On the way they attacked a stronghold of al-Kamil at Mansurah but they were defeated and forced to surrender. The terms of the surrender included the retreat from Damietta, getting out of Egypt, and an eight-year truce. The Fifth Crusade thus ended in a Crusader defeat that failed to achieve its goals.

In April 1213, Innocent III issued his papal bull Quia Maior which called on all of Christendom to join a new Crusade calling again for the recovery of the Holy Land. Innocent wanted it to be led by the papacy which he believed the First Crusade should have been, to avoid the errors of the Fourth Crusade, which had been taken over by the Venetians.

Innocent III died on the 16th of July 1216 and Honorius III was consecrated as pope the following week. The Crusade dominated the early part of his papacy and the next year, he crowned Peter II of Courtenay as Latin Emperor, but he was captured in Epirus and died in confinement.

Robert of Courçon was despached as spiritual advisor to the French fleet but he was subordinate to newly-chosen papal delegate named Pelagius of Albano.

The strength of the armies was estimated at more

than thirty-two thousand, including more than ten thousand knights and the departure of the Crusaders began finally in early July 1217. Many of the Crusaders decided to go to the Holy Land by a sea journey and the fleet made their first stop at Dartmouth on the southern coast of England. From there, led by William I of Holland, they continued south to Lisbon in Portugal.

At their arrival in Portugal, the Bishop of Lisbon attempted to persuade the Crusaders to help them capture the Almohad controlled city of Alcácer do Sal. Some members of the fleet were convinced by the Portuguese and started the siege of Alcácer do Sal in August 1217. The Crusaders eventually captured the city with the help of the Knights Templar and Knights Hospitaller in October 1217.

A group of Frisians who refused to aid the Portuguese with their siege plans against Alacácer do Sal, raided several coastal towns on their way to the Holy Land. They attacked Faro, Rota, Cádiz and Ibiza stealing loot in abundance. They thereafter followed the coast of southern France and wintered in Civitavecchia in Italy in 1217 and 1218, before continuing on their journey to Acre.

Innocent III had secured the participation of the Kingdom of Georgia in the Crusade. Under the rule of Queen Tamar, Georgia challenged Ayyubid rule in eastern Anatolia. Tamar died in 1213 and was succeeded by her son George IV of Georgia. Late 1210, according to the Georgian chronicles, he commenced preparations for a campaign in the Holy Land in support of the Franks but his plans were cut short by the invasion of the Mongols in 1220. After his death, his sister Rusudan of Georgia notified the pope that Georgia was unable to fulfill its promises.

After Saladin died in 1193 he was succeeded by his brother al-Adil and Saladin's son, az-Zahir Ghazi, kept control on Aleppo.

Following seaborne raids on Rosetta in 1204 and Damietta in 1211, the primary concern of al-Adil included Egypt. Willing to agree on concessions to avoid war, he favoured the Italian states of Venice and Pisa, both for trading benefits and to avoid having them giving support to further crusades. The biggest part of his sultanship was carried out whilst under truces with the Christians. He had a new fortress at Mount Tabor built in order to strengthen the defences of Jerusalem and Damascus. The majority of his conflicts in Syria were with the Knights Hospitaller at Krak des Chevaliers or with Bohemond IV of Antioch and these were dealt with by his nephew az-Zahir Ghazi. Just one time, in 1207, did he choose outright confrontation the Crusaders when captured al-Qualai'ah, besieged Krak des Chevaliers and advanced to Tripoli, before accepting compensation from Bohemond IV in exchange for peace.

Az-Zahir kept up an alliance with both Antioch and the sultan of Rûm, to balance the influence of Leo I of Armenia but he died in 1216, leaving as his successor al-Aziz Muhammad, his three-year-old son. Saladin's eldest son, al-Afdal, made a bid for Aleppo by enlisting the assistance of Kaykaus I. In 1218, al-Afdal and Kaykaus invaded Aleppo and advanced on the capital. The problem was solved when al-Ashraf, al-Adil's third son, defeated the Seljuk army. Considereing the Crusaders' Egyptian plan, these diversions were of good use since they stretched the resources of the sultanate that controlled the Levant.

The leader to to take up the cross first in the Fifth Crusade was King Andrew II of Hungary who had been called apon by the pope to oblige his father's vow to lead a crusade. He eventually agreed after he had postponed it three times previously. Andrew, who had a reputation for wanting tobecome Latin emperor himself, raised fund from his estates to finance the Crusade. During July 1217, the Hungarian king departed from Zagreb, escorted by Leopold VI of Austria plus Otto I, Duke of Merania.

King Andrew's army, being around twenty thousand mounted soldiers and even more infantrymen, many of them stayed behind when Andrew embarked in Split, Croatia, two months later. With transportation laid on by the large Venetian fleet, Andrew and his troops embarked from Split on the 23rd of August 1217.

The Hungarian army made land on Cyprus in October 1217 and sailed from there to Acre to join John of Brienne, Raoul of Merencourt and Hugh I of Cyprus.

Up until he returned to Hungary, King Andrew remained in leadership of Christian forces of the Fifth Crusade. That October, the chieftains of the enterprise held a war council there which was presided by Andrew II. Additionally in attendance was Leopold VI of Austria, Otto I of Merania, Walter II of Avesnes, and numerous archbishops and bishops.

The war plan of the Emperor of Constantinople, John of Brienne, anticipated a two-pronged attack; in Syria, crusader forces would engage al-Mu'azzam, son of Al-Adil, at the fortress of Nablus and, simultaneously, the fleet would attack the port city of Damietta, snatching Egypt from the power of the Muslims thus enabling the conquest of the rest of Palestine and Syria. This plan, however, was abandoned at Acre, because of too few fighting men and boats. As an alternative whilst in hope of reinforcements, the short-term objective became to keep the enemy occupied until a more opportune time arose, in a series of smaller engagements.

The Muslims suspected that the Crusaders were coming in 1216 because of the exodus of merchants from Alexandria. Once the crusaders grouped at Acre, Al-Adil commenced operations in Syria and left the larger part of his forces in Egypt under his eldest son Al-Kamil. He did, however, personally led a small contingent to support al-Mu'azzam, emir of Damascus. With not enough men to fully engage the Crusaders, he guarded the approaches to Damascus while al- Mu'azzam was despatched to Nablus so as to protect Jerusalem.

The Crusaders were camped at Tel Afek, near Acre and on the 3rd of November 1217 they began to cross the plain of Esdraelon in the direction of 'Ain Jalud, but they expected an ambush. When they witnessed the strength of the Crusaders, al-Adil withdrew to Beisan even though this was against the wishes of al-Mu'azzam who wished to attack from the heights of Nain. Once more, against the wishes of his son, Al-Adil abandoned Beisan which quickly fell to the Crusaders who then pillaged the city.

Al-Adil continued his retreat to Ajlun, whilst ordering al-Mu'azzam to protect Jerusalem from the heights of Lubban, near Shiloh, then he continued to Damascus, stopping only at Marj al-Saffar.

On the 10th of November 1217, the Crusaders crossed the Jordan River at the Jisr el-Majami, from where they were threatening Damascus. The governor of the city took defensive measures, and received reinforcements from al-Mujahid Shirkuh, the Ayyubid emir of Homs. Not then engaging the Muslims, the Crusaders returned to their camp near Acre.

Supported by Bohemond IV and under the command of John of Brienne, the King of Jerusalem, the Hungarians moved against Mount Tabor, thought of by the Muslims as unassailable. A battle fought during December 1217 was soon abandoned. Met with the incendiary weapon known as Greek fire, the siege was abandoned on the 7th of December 1217. A third raid by the Hungarians, led by Andrew's nephew, was thwarted at Mashghara. The small force was demolished andthe few survivors returned to Acre that Christmas Eve, ending the Hungarian Crusade of 1217.

At the start of 1218, and under the threat of excommunication, an ailing Andrew chose to return to Hungary. In the meantime, efforts were taken to strengthen Château Pèlerin, proving valuable actions later on. Later in the year, Oliver of Paderborn arrived with a fresh army and William I of Holland came with an army of Dutch, Flemish and Frisian soldiers. The campaign was to be led by John of Brienne, because on his status in the kingdom and his military reputation. The previous objective, dropped the year before because of shortages in resources, was reinvigorated. The plan to attack Egypt was made, an early assault on Jerusalem excluded because of excessive heat and water shortages. The crusaders focused their main attack on the port of Damietta rather than Alexandria.

At the end of May 1218, the first of the Crusader's fleet arrived at the harbour of Damietta. Simon III of Sarrebrück was made temporary leader pending the arrival of the remainder of the fleet, but, within a few days, the rest of the ships arrived, carrying John of Brienne, Leopold VI of Austria and masters Peire de Montagut, Hermann of Salza and Guérin de Montaigu.

The Muslims showed little alarm at the arrival of the Crusaders, thinking that they would be success in mounting an attack on Egypt. Al-Adil had supported peace treaties when more radical elements in the sultanate had sought jihad. He was camped at Marj al-Saffar, and his sons al-Kamil and al-Mu'azzam were given the task of defending Cairo and the Syrian coast from Syria, and an Egyptian force were encamped at al-'Adiliyah, some miles south of Damietta. The Egyptians were not strong enough to attack the Crusaders but served instead to oppose any invader attempt from across the Nile.

The siege of Damietta commenced on the 23rd of June 1218 with an assault on the tower, using more tan eighty ships, some with catapaulting machines, but with little success. The first ship to attack was forced to withdraw when up against concentrated counter-barrage. Scaling ladders tied against the walls collapsed due to the weight of the soldiers and the first attempt at an assault ended in failure. Near the end of August a renewed assault was commenced and on the second day the tower was taken and its defensive chains severed.

The loss of the chain tower was vastly shocking for the Ayyubids and the sultan al-Adil died shortly after this event and was succeeded by his son al-Kamil.

The Crusaders did not fully exploit their advantage and many prepared to return home, now having regarded their vows as crusaders to be fulfilled. Further offensive action was then stalled until the Nile River was more favourable and the arrival of additional forces was gratified. Among them were papal legate Pelagius Galvani and his aide Robert of Courçon, who travelled with a group of Roman Crusaders paid for by the pope. A group further from England shortly after arrived, led by Ranulf de Blondeville and Oliver and Richard who were both illegitimate sons of King John.

On the 9th of October 1218, Egyptian forces made a surprise attack on the Crusaders' camp. Seeing their intentions, John of Brienne and his men attacked and crushed the Egyptian advance guard which impeded the main force.

From the initial stages, Pelagius judged himself to be the supreme commander of the Crusade, then, because he was powerless to launch a major offensive, he despatched specially equipped ships up the Nile River, but this gave no advantage.

The Crusaders next built a large floating fortress on the river, but a storm blew up sending it near the Egyptian camp. The Egyptians seized the fortress, killing all of its defenders apart from two soldiers who were then accused of cowardice and their execution was ordered by John. In the months following, diseases killed many of the Crusaders, including Robert of Courçon. During a storm, Pelagius took over leadership of the expedition and the Crusaders supported this, wanting a new, more aggressive leadership.

Concurrently, al-Kamil, commanding the defenders, was almost overthrown by a coup to replace him with his younger brother al-Faiz Ibrahim. Alerted to the conspiracy, al-Kamil fled the camp and in the confusion that followed, the Crusaders were able to advance on Damietta.

The Crusaders surrounded Damietta, with the Italians to the north, Templars and Hospitallers to the east, and John of Brienne with his French and Pisan troops to the south. The Frisians and Germans occupied a nearby camp and a new wave of reinforcements from Cyprus arrived led by Walter III of Caesarea.

At this point, al-Kamil and al-Mu'azzam tried to open negotiations with the Crusaders and asked Christian envoys to come to their camp. They offered to surrender Jerusalem, but not al-Karak and Krak de Montréal which guarded to road to Egypt. Also offered was a multi-year truce, these things in exchange for the Crusaders' evacuation of Egypt. John of Brienne and the other leaders liked the offer since the original objective of the Crusade was the recovery of Jerusalem. But Pelagius and the leaders of the Templars, Hospitallers and Venetians refused this and a subsequent offer. Al-Mu'azzam responded by reorganizing his reinforcements at Fariskur.

In the Holy Land, al-Mu'azzam's forces began dismantling fortifications at Mount Tabor and other defensive positions, including Jerusalem, in order to weaken them should the Crusaders prevail there. Al-Muzaffar II Mahmud, the son of the Ayyubid emir of Hama, arrived in Egypt with Syrian reinforcements, leading multiple attacks on the Crusader camp but with limited impact. Meanwhile Crusaders including Leopold VI of Austria returned to Europe, but their loss was more than offset by replacements who included Guy I Embriaco, who also brought urgently needed supplies.

Muslim attacks continued through May, and also Crusader counter-attacks. Despite objections from the military leaders, Pelagius began multiple attacks on the city using Pisan and Venetian troops but each time they were repelled by the defenders who used Greek fire. A counter-offensive by the Egyptians on the Templar camp was repulsed by their new leader

Peire de Montagut and supported by the Teutonic Knights. An attack on the sultan's camp at Fariskur at the end of August led by Pelagius was a disaster which resulted in high losses for the Crusaders.

In the August of 1219, the sultan, using recent captives as envoys to the Christians, again offered peace. His offerings included earlier provisions in addition to paying for the rebuilding of the damaged fortifications plus the release of prisoners and the return of the section of the True Cross lost at the battle of Hattin but again, his offer was rejected. However, Pelagius' hope that victory was attainable was boosted by the continued arrival of new crusaders.

During the September of 1219, Francis of Assisi, who had an extensive history with the Crusades, arrived in the Crusader camp and sought permission from Pelagius to pay a visit to sultan al-Kamil.

Initially turning down this request, Pelagius did grant Francis and his companion, Illuminato da Rieti, his permission to go, even though he thought it to be a suicide mission. The two men went over to preach to al-Kamil, who, however, assumed that they were emissaries of the Crusaders and received them politely. When he realised that their intention was to preach against Islam, many in his court wanted to see the execution of the friars. Al-Kamil did, however, hear them out before having them accompanied back to the Crusader encampment.

Francis obtained a commitment for more humane treatment for Christian captives from the sultan. He remained in Egypt whilst the fall of Damietta happened and departed then to Acre. While in Acre he established the Province of the Holy Land and a priory of the Franciscan Order.

With the negotiations with the Crusaders stalled and Damietta isolated, later in November 1219 al-Kamil despatched a re-supply convoy through the sector manned by the troops of Hervé IV of Donzy. The Egyptians were mostly stopped but the intrusion re-inspired the Crusaders with a unity of purpose.

On the 5th of November 1219 the Crusaders entered Damietta and found it largely abandoned. With Christian banners flying over the city, al-Kamil moved his men from Fariskur downriver to Mansurah. Survivors in Damietta were either sent into slavery or held as hostages for trading for Christian prisoners.

By the 23rd of November 1219, the Crusaders had captured the neighbouring city of Tinnis, at the mouth of the Nile, giving them access to the food bounties of Lake Manzala.

There was disagreement as to who should the rule Damietta but after John of Brienne prepared to leave in frustration, Pelagius relented and allowed him to lead Damietta provided an agreement by the pope was made. However, the Italians, wanting a bigger share of the booty, took up arms and drove the French from the city. Not until the beginning of February 1220 did the situation calm down and a formal ceremony was held to celebrate the Christian victory. John of Brienne shortly after departed since pope Honorius III had decided Damietta's leadership in favour of his ambassador Pelagius.

Leo I of Armenia, who was the father-in-law of John of Brienne, died on the beginning of May 1219 which left his succession in doubt. John had a claim to the Armenian throne which was through his wife Stephanie of Armenia but Leo I had left the kingdom to his infant daughter, Isabella. The pope dictated in February 1220 that John was the rightful heir to the Armenian Kingdom of Cilicia.

John went Jerusalem near the Eastertime of 1220 so that he could assert his claim to his inheritance, but Stephanie and their son died shortly after his arrival, ending his claim to Cilicia. When the pope learned of the deaths, he announced Raymond-Roupen, whom Leo I had disinherited, to be the approved ruler and threatened John with excommunication if he put up a fight for Cilicia. In order to consolidate his position, Raymond-Roupen went to Damietta in the summer of 1220 to meet with Pelagius.

Following the capture of Damietta, Walter of Caesarea brought one hundred Cypriote knights plus their soldiers, and including a Cypriote knight named

Peter Chappe with his charge, a young Philip of Novara. In John's absence, Pelagius left the sea routes between Damietta and Acre insufficiently guarded. Taking advantage of this, a Muslim fleet attacked the Crusaders in the port of Limassol causing more than one thousand Christian casualties.

The majority of the Cypriotes left Egypt at the same time as John but, when he returned, he passed through Cyprus and brought further forces with him.

John remained in Jerusalem for some months, restricted by lack of funds but he returned to Egypt and re-joined the Crusade in early July 1221 at the command of the pope.

Around this time, al-Kamil sent Fakhr ad-Din ibn as-Shaikh on an delegation to the court of al-Kamil's brother, al-Ashraf, then ruling greater Armenia from a base in Sinjar, to ask for assistance in fighting the Crusaders but he was initially turned down. Also, at this time, the Muslims were also threatened by the Mongols in Persia, who at that time had not yet converted to Islam. When Abbasid caliph al-Nasir requested troops from al-Ashraf, he instead sent them to assist his brother in Egypt. The Ayyubids found that the events that followed allowed them to focus on the invaders at Damietta.

In the captured city, Pelagius was unable to raise the Crusaders from inactivity throughout the year of 1220, except for a Templar raiding party on Burlus that July. The Crusaders pillaged the town but suffered the loss and capture of numerous knights. The calmer times in Egypt enabled al-Mu'azzam who had returned to Syria after the defeat at Damietta, to attack the remaining coastal strongholds and to take Caesarea.

At this time, Al-Kamil took an advantage and reinforced Mansurah to make it into a fortified city, replacing Damietta as the main protection at the mouth of the Nile. He also renewed his peace offering to the Crusaders but again it was refused. Pelagius' view was that he was holding the key to conquering both Egypt and Jerusalem.

During the December of 1220, Honorius III proclaimed that Frederick II would be sending troops, expected by March 1221. Substantial contingents of troops arrived that May which were led by Louis I of Bavaria and his bishop, Ulrich II of Passau but they were under orders not to begin offensive operations until after Frederick arrived.

The Crusaders had become aware of writings, in Arabic, which claimed to have predicted Saladin's earlier capture of Jerusalem and the Christian capture of Damietta. Because of these writings and other prophesies, fears arose amongst the Muslims of a Christian uprising against the power of Islam, this situation partly influencing al-Kamil's peace considerations.

In July 1221, new began circulating that the army of a King David, was on its way from the east to the Holy Land to join the Crusade and to get the release of the sultan's Christian captives. This news created excitement among the Crusaders and this influenced them to hurriedly launch an attack on Cairo.

Meanwhile, on the 4th July, Pelagius, having decided to advance to the south, instructed a three-day fast in preparation for the movement. John of Brienne, arriving in Egypt shortly afterwards, opinioned against the move, but was helpless to halt it. Now thought a traitor for opposing these plans and also faced with the threat of excommunication, John of Brienne merged with the force under the command of the emissary. They moved onwards towards Fariskur on the twelfth of July to where Pelagius drew the forces up into battle formation.

The Crusaders advanced to Sharamsah, mid-way between Fariskur and Mansurah which was on the east bank of the Nile River and occupied the city on that twelfth of July. On the twenty-fourth of July, Pelagius moved his forces near the al-Bahr as-Saghit, south of the village of Ashmun al-Rumman, which was on the opposite bank from Mansurah. He had planned to sustain supply lines with Damietta, since insufficient food for his large army had been brought with them.

Their fortifications were somewhat inadequate

and the situation for the Crusaders made more dangerous because of the reinforcements the Egyptians brought in from Syria. Alice of Cyprus and other leaders of military orders warned Pelagius of the increasingly big numbers of Muslim fighters arriving and ongoing warnings from John of Brienne were overlooked. Large numbers of Crusaders then took their opportunity to retreat back to Damietta and later departed to their home countries.

The Egyptians had a clear advantage of being familiar with the terrain, particularly knowing the canals which ran close to the Crusader camp. On a canal near Barāmūn, which could support large vessels, and during late August when the Nile was at its highest, the Egyptians brought numerous ships up from al-Maḥallah. Coming into the Nile, they were able to intercept the Crusaders' supply lines from Damietta, making their position unsustainable.

On the 26th of August 1221, the Crusaders tried to reach Barāmūn whilst in night-time darkness, but the Egyptians were alerted and harrassed them. In the meantime, al-Kamil had channels along the bank of the Nile opened which flooded the area making battle untenable. Two days later, Pelagius tried again for peace, and sent an envoy to al-Kamil.

The Crusaders however, still had a strong position, with Damietta being well-garrisoned and a naval fleet under Henry of Malta, Sicilian Walter of

Palearia and German Anselm of Justingen, all having been sent by Frederick II. They offered the sultan withdrawal from Damietta and an eight-year truce in exchange for allowing the pass of the Crusader army, plus the release of all prisoners, and also the return of the relic of the True Cross.

The news of the surrender was sent to Damietta but It was ill-received, with the Venetians attempting to gain control. But however, the Crusader ships departed, and the sultan entered the city, thus the Fifth Crusade was over.

THE SIXTH CRUSADE

The Sixth Crusade carried out between 1228 and 1229 AD, and also known as the Crusade of Frederick II, was another military expedition to recapture Jerusalem and the remainder of the Holy Land. It commenced seven years after the conclusion of the Fifth Crusade and involved minimal actual fighting. The ambassadorial manipulations of the Holy Roman Emperor and King of Sicily, Frederick II, resulted in the Kingdom of Jerusalem and the retrieval of control over the city of Jerusalem for most of the following fifteen years and also over other parts of the Holy Land.

Once again, preachers were despatched right across Europe to gather support for a fresh crusade, this time to be led by Frederick II. Although transport ships were being made ready, the target date was looking unlikely to be met. Hermann of Salza and Raoul of Mérencourt went to the pope to update him on the progress. Honorius III commanded cardinal bishop Conrad of Porto as papal legate to Germany. There pressing the clergy there to continue to pursue the crusade. The pope also urged King Louis VIII of France to join Frederick II, and to resolve a quarrel with Raymond VII of Toulouse. Despite all of this, the efforts were not getting much in results, making the timetable set at Ferentino appear non-achievable. The pope reluctantly agreed to a postpone -ment only a few days before the agreed deadline and ten years after Frederick had first committed to the crusade.

The Agreement was signed between Frederick II and Honorius III. Frederick promised to depart on the Crusade by the fifteenth of August 1227 and remain for two years and to maintain one thousand knights in Syria, also to provide transport for additional forces, and to give to Rome a hundred thousand ounces in gold, funds which would be returned to Frederick after he had arrived at Acre. Should he fail to arrive, the gold would be used for future requirements of the Holy Land.

Frederick also guaranteed that on going on Crusade that he would lead it. After the agreement was signed, Guala became Bishop of Brescia. Moreover, based on the terms of the agreement, all papal possessions in the Kingdom of Sicily were to be restored to the pope.

Frederick agreed to the terms of the pope at the high altar with his hand on the Gospels. In a letter to the pope, he reiterated the terms and accepted the punishments threatened in the event that the Crusade was not carried out, therefore, committing himself beyond all reversal of his promise.

Frederick II wanted to go to the Holy Land as king of Jerusalem. He married John of Brienne's daughter Isabella II by proxy in August 1225 and fulfilling John of Brienne's wishes, Isabella was crowned queen of Jerusalem a few days later at Tyre. Frederick sent fourteen ships to collect her and they were formally married at Brindisi on the 9th of November 1227.

John and Frederick's family relationship became soured, since Frederick claimed the kingship of Jerusalem while John had supposedly been guaranteed that he would be king of Jerusalem for the remainder of his life. Frederick however claimed that John had forfeited his entitlement to the kingdom when Isabella married him and proclaimed himself king of Jerusalem in the December of 1225.

John of Brienne travelled to Rome, where he received sympathy from pope Honorius. Many important people in Jurusalem, however, acknowledged Frederick as their proper king. The law, however, the Assizes of Jerusalem, required that the king to be a resident of the kingdom.

The treasure of the kingdom was depleted, and additional funds were badly needed. The conciliar decree Ad Liberandam formulated a system of public financing for Crusades and some of these funds went directly to local Crusaders.

By the start of 1220, Innocent III had established distribution but Frederick did not benefit from it and for the next few years there was limited ecclesiastical funds directed toward his planned Crusade, the funding for this Sixth Crusade needing to be raised by the emperor himself. Frederick executed a levy on Sicily and also gained financial support from Cyprus but limited funds did also limit the size of his Crusader army.

In 1226 it had become apparent that the Sixth Crusade would begin with an invasion of Syria and Palestine again with the objective of conquering Jerusalem. Following the death of Honorius III in 1227, the new pope Gregory IX entered the Crusader proceedings.

The first groups of Crusaders, including Germans under the command of Thomas of Aquino and Henry of Limburg, and French and English under the command of the bishops Peter des Roches and William Briwere, set sail in August 1227 and got to Syria in early October. After they arrived at Acre, they joined with forces of the kingdom and better secured the coastal towns of Caesarea and Jaffa. They also coerced the Muslims out of Sidon and fortified the island of Qal'at al-Bahr. The Germans also rebuilt Montfort Castle, which was to the northeast of Acre, for the Teutonic Knights.

The emperor and his men were delayed while their ships were refitted but they did finally sail on the 8th of September 1227. However, before they reached their first stop of Otranto, Frederick, and many others, contracted the plague. Frederick came ashore to seek better medical attention, and, resolving to keep his oath, he sent a fleet of twenty ships on to Acre which included in command, Hermann of Salza, Gérold of Lausanne, Odo of Montbéliard and Balian of Sidon. The Crusade, however, was now under the overall command of Henry IV, Duke of Limburg.

Frederick II sent his messengers to inform Gregory IX of the developments but the pope declined to meet with them or to hear Frederick's side of the story. Frederick II, the Holy Roman Emperor, was excommunicated at the end of September 1227.

The pope did not give consideration to Frederick's illness, only caring that he had not kept his agreement. In a circular letter announcing the excommunication, Frederick was branded a wanton violator of his sacred oath, was held responsible for the deaths of Crusaders at Brindisi and was accused of feigning his illness.

In November 1227, an emissary of the sultan, was sent to meet with the emperor. The negotiations were carried out in secret which caused concern amongst the German Crusaders. Soon after, the emperor's negotiator sent word that al-Mu'azzam had suddenly died, a revelation changing the balance of power. Frederick then sent the marshal of the Kingdom of Sicily, to Syria with five hundred knights to augment to force already there while he was preparing for a departure in the spring of 1228.

Frederick made one final effort to be reconciled with pope Gregory, sending Albert I of Käfernburg, the archbishop of Magdeburg, and two Sicilian justiciars to speak with him but to no effect. Frederick sailed from Brindisi near the end of June 1228, the fleet under the command of admiral Henry of Malta, only a comparatively small force going, since the main force had sailed in August 1227.

The route of Frederick's fleet is recorded. it stopped in Otranto, then across the Adriatic Sea to the island of Othonoi. Then was in Corfu, then Porto Guiscardo in Cephalonia in the beginning of July, Methoni a few days later, then Portocaglie near Cape Matapan, then Cerigo before it reached Souda Bay on Crete. The fleet moved slowly along the Cretan coast, pausing for a whole day at Heraklion before crossing the Aegean Sea to Rhodes around the middle of July. They sailed along the coast to Phenika, where they stayed to replenish the freshwater stocks. The fleet next sailed across to Cyprus where they arrived at Limassol.

Cyprus had been an Imperial fiefdom since the emperor Henry VI, Frederick's father, had been made king on the eve of the 1196 German Crusade.

Frederick sailed to Acre from Famagusta near the beginning of September, 1228, accompanied by king

Henry I of Cyprus, John of Ibelin, and various Cypriote noblemen. He arrived in Acre on the 7th of September 1228 and was greeted warmly by the Templars, Hospitallers and the clergy. However, he was denied the kiss of peace due to his excommunication. Yielding to pressure, he made overtures to the pope and sent both Henry of Malta and archbishop Marino Filangieri to announce his arrival in Syria and, in addition, to request absolution. Gregory IX, however, had already made his decision and sent word to the Latin patriarch and masters of the military orders that Frederick's excommunication still held, despite his eventual arrival.

Frederick did not immediately take action since Acre was split in its support for him. His own army and the Teutonic Knights supported him but the Templars and the Syrian clergy followed the hostile papal line. Once news of Frederick's excommunication had spread, public support for him waned considerably.

Frederick's army was not large since the troops he had sent under duke Henry of Limburg in 1227 had mostly returned home out of impatience or of fear of offending the Church.Even augmented with the forces available in Outremer, he was unable to gather an effective army capable of striking a decisive blow against the Muslims. This meant that he could not afford nor mount a lengthening campaign in the Holy Land and the Sixth Crusade would be one of negotiation.

Frederick realised that his main hope of success in the Holy Land lay in negotiation for the return of Jerusalem since he lacked the manpower to engage in effective battle. He therefore sent emmisionaries to inform the sultan of his arrival in the Holy Land and in reply, he received the ambassadors of the sultan, including Fakhr ad-Din ibn as-Shaikh, at the Hospitaller camp at Recordane, near Acre.

The treaty was concluded on the 18th of February 1229 which involved a ten-year truce and the English bishops Peter des Roches and William Bri were witness to the signing.

Frederick went into Jerusalem during the middle of March 1229 and was given the official surrender of the city by al-Kamil's agent then he crowned himself in the Church of the Holy Sepulchre. Wearing his crown, Frederick continued to the palace of the Hospitallers where he met with bishops and military personnel to discuss the fortifications of the city.

The expiry after ten years of Frederick's treaty with al-Kamil provoked Pope Gregory IX to call for another crusade to make the Holy Lands secure for Christendom beyond 1239. This set the scene for the Barons' Crusade, a poorly organized enterprise which gained little support from either Frederick or the pope, but which however recovered more land from the Muslims than the Sixth Crusade.

THE BARONS' CRUSADE

The Barons' Crusade of 1239, was a crusade to the Holy Land which, in terms of gaining territory, was the crusade with the greatest success since the First Crusade. It was called by Pope Gregory IX, and widely expressed the zenith of papal undertaking to make crusading a universal Christian enterprise.

The Sixth Crusade had been vehemently unpopular amongst the local Christian leaders because the excommunicated Frederick had left them defenceless and allied with their Muslim enemies. They also recognised his attempt to gain control over the Holy Land for the House of Hohenstaufen rather than give back territory to local barons of the Kingdom of Jerusalem.

In 1234, Pope Gregory IX announced that a new crusade would be launched in the Holy Land in the following five years. This in order to safeguard Christian control and his effort to unite Christians to defend the Holy Land, he issued a papal bull which was vigorously used by begging friars to promote the crusade all over the Christian domains.

To make the crusade widespread, Gregory asked

for all Christians to attend crusade sermons and donate sums of money, suggesting one penny per week for ten years.

Around twelve months later, in December 1235, Gregory began attempting to redirect the planned crusade away from the Holy Land to instead combat the spread of Christian heresy in Latin Greece but was largely unsuccessful. The Latin emperor, John of Brienne, who was the most energetic papal supporter out of the associated rulers, allowed in Constantinople the authority of a Latin leader, a situation which suggested a possibility of unifying both Greek and Latin churches.

The Hungarian military elite headed by its king refused to go to Constantinople to fight the invaders headed by, John III of Nicaes and Ivan II of Bulgaria. In the summer of 1239, Hungarian king Béla allowed Baldwin of Courtenay to cross the Hungarian border but declined to join him on his way to Constantinople.

Around this time, Pope Gregory relayed a letter to the Dominicans' prior in Hungary requesting his preaching of the cross within the empire and for the exchange vows for Jerusalem given by crusaders on those to Constantinople in return for absolution. The pope promised absolution to every soldier as well as to anyone who contributed funding to the crusade. During that February of 1241, Gregory instructed the redirection of the revenues collected in Hungary to a fresh military campaign against Frederic II, the German emperor.

Baldwin of Courtenay, got to Constantinople first while other non-unified European knights and nobility, moved on in the direction of Jerusalem. In 1235, Gregory put out a request to French crusaders to fight in Constantinople rather than the Holy Land. On that sixteenth of December, the pope instructed the Franciscan William of Cordelle to preach for a crusade in Latin Greece.Theobald did however receive funding from Gregory for his crusade to Jerusalem and the fragmented groups of French barons travelled separately to the Holy Land where in due course they had some degree of military defeat but followed by some diplomatic success. The English barons, including Richard of Cornwall and Simon of Montfort finally arrived there one year later.

Theobald I, the king of French Navarre, gathered a striking collection of European nobles at Lyon which included Hugh IV, Duke of Burgundy; Amaury VI of Montfort; Robert de Courtenay the Grand Butler of France, and Peter I, Duke of Brittany. These high nobles were accompanied by a number of lesser nobility which included Guigues IV of Forez, Henry II, Count of Bar, Louis of Sancerre, Jehan de Braine the Count of Mâcon, William of Joigny, and Henry of Grandpré. Theobald's main army contained around fifteen hundred knights. They left from France in

August 1239, with the majority sailing from Marseilles and others departing from Frederick II's ports in the South of Italy. Theobald got to Acre at the beginning of September and was soon joined by other crusaders who had been scuttled by a Mediterranean storm whilst on their way.

Once there, they were received by a council of local Christian leaders who included Walter of Brienne, Odo of Montbéliard, Balian of Beirut, John of Arsuf, and Balian of Sidon and they were also joined by further crusaders who had come from Cyprus.

Eventually, at the beginning of that November, the assembly of approximately four thousand knights, those being more than fifty percent from the local barons and military orders, marched on to Ascalon, where they began to initiate the reconstruction of a castle which had been demolished decades before by Saladin's hordes.

After two days of marching, Peter of Brittany and his lieutenant Raoul de Soissons divided off to make a raid. They split their forces and each waited hoping to ambush a Muslim caravan which was moving up the Jordan valley to Damascus. Peter's men clashed with the Muslims outside a castle, and after fierce fighting, he sounded a horn to summon Raoul. The Muslims were overwhelmed and ran away inside the castle. Peter's men followed them in where they killed many, took some captive and looted the valuables and the animals fit for food from the caravan.

Peter's small victory would soon be put into the shadow when the whole army reached Jaffa on the 12th of November and a section of the army desired to conduct a raid of their own. They were led by Henry of Bar, Amaury of Montfort, and Hugh of Burgundy, as well as four of the major local lords. This assembly who included up to six hundred knights, split off from the main force and going against the clear protestations of Theobald, Peter of Brittany, and the leaders of the military orders, these being, the Knights Templar, the Knights Hospitaller, and the Teutonic Order. The assembly rode their horses all night and a section of them later battled an Egyptian force commanded by Rukn al-Din al-Hijawi at the battle at Gaza during the following day which happened to be the 13th of November. The crusader group was securely defeated before Theobald's forces could get there to support them. Henry was killed, and Amaury was one among several hundred other crusaders who were taken prisoner. The army then retreated right the way back to Acre.

Around a month after the battle at Gaza, an-Nasir Dawud of Transjordan, whose caravan had been attacked by Peter's men, sent his men towards Jerusalem, which was then weakly defended, and there laid siege. After one month of being cooped up there, the garrison of the citadel surrendered to Dawud on the seventh of December after accepting the offer of safe passage to Acre. This left Jerusalem in Muslim occupation for the first time since 1229 during the Sixth Crusade.

After the crusaders' misfortunate conclusion at Gaza plus the loss of Jerusalem, an internal war within the Muslim Ayyubid dynasty started to provide a lucky looking situation for the Christians. However, the emir Al-Muzaffar II Mahmud of Hama wished to distract his enemy, Al-Mujahid of Homs, so he lured Theobald's crusaders to Pilgrim Mountain outside of Tripoli with inconclusive offerings, but nothing happened since the crusaders had returned to Acre by early May 1240.

The Crusader's following encounter with the Ayyubids turned out to be decisively more beneficial.

Theobald negotiated with the warring emirs of Damascus and Egypt and he finalized a agreement with the As-Salih Ismail, Emir of Damascus in the north, which worked against the Ayyub of Egypt, whereby the Kingdom of Jerusalem regained Jerusalem itself, plus Bethlehem, Nazareth, and most of the region of Galilee with many Templar castles, including Beaufort and Saphet.

However, Ismail's treaty with the crusaders included a lot of territory that was not really his to give, but it was in recognition rights to take Dawud's lands. This treaty was grossly unpopular with Ismail's own subjects and the influential preacher Abd al-Salam publicly denounced it but Ismail had Ibn 'Abd al-Salam arrested in retaliation. In a show of even more intense protestations, the Muslim garrison of Beaufort refused to hand over the castle to Balian of Sidon, as Ismail's accord required. Ismail himself found it nesessary to besiege the stronghold with an army from Damascus for several months in order to seize it for the Crusaders who, meanwhile, set about pursuing their claims to Dawud's lands. They began the rebuilding of Ascalon and carried out raids throughout the Jordan valley, eventually retaking Jerusalem and attacking Nablus. This put pressure on Dawud to negotiate his treaty with Theobald in the summer of 1240 and fulfilled in action many of the concessions which Ismail had had granted only in theory.

Theobald and Peter of Brittany did not remain to see their agreements with Ismail of Damascus and Dawud of Transjordan fully carried out since they departed from Palestine for Europe in mid-September 1240 in advance of Richard of Cornwall arrival, apparently because they wanted to avoid being present during further internal quarrelling over the leadership and direction of the enterprise.

It was on the 10th of June 1240 that Richard, 1st Earl of Cornwall, left England with a modest sized army of crusaders. This assembly was made up of around twelve English barons and several hundred knights, including William II Longespée. They travelled to Marseilles in the South of France during the September of 1240 and got to Acre on the 8th of October. Following that, William of Forz organized the third successful expedition to Jerusalem.

Richard and the other crusaders did not enter any combat but, however, they completed negotiations for a truce with Ayyubid leaders originally made by Theobald not many months before, when in the initial wave of the crusade. They then continued with the rebuilding of Ascalon castle, and, remarkably, Richard handed over custody of it to Walter Pennenpié, the conspicuous agent of Frederick II of Jerusalem, when he could have handed it over to the local liege men of the Kingdom of Jerusalem who vehemently opposed

Frederick's rule. On the 23rd of April 1241 an exchange of Muslim prisoners for Christian captives was carried out, most remarkably, Simon's older brother Amaury, who had been captured during Henry of Bar's disastrous raid at Gaza eighteen months earlier. They also moved the remains of those fallen in that battle and interred them at the cemetery in Ascalon. His work completed, Richard left Acre to return to England on the 3rd of May 1241.

Even though the Barons' Crusade returned the

Kingdom of Jerusalem to its largest size since 1187, the successes would be severely put into reverse only a few years later. On the 15th of July 1244, Jerusalem was not only captured but was diminished to ruination during the Siege of Jerusalem of 1244 when its Christians were massacred by Khwarazmians from northern Syria who were new allies of the Sultan of Egypt, As-Salih Ayyub. In another few months on in October, 1244, Ayyub and the Khwarazmian forces achieved a major military victory at the Battle of La Forbie. This had a permanent crippling effect on Christian military power in the Holy Land which took its toll for years to come.

THE SEVENTH CRUSADE

The crusade from 1248 to 1254, the Seventh Crusade, was the first of the two Crusades led by French King, Louis IX and aimed to reclaim the Holy Land by attacking Egypt, the principle bastion of Muslim power in the Near East. The Crusade was launched in response to the loss of the Holy City of Jerusalem in 1244. It was preached by pope Innocent IV in conjunction with a crusade against emperor Frederick II as well as Baltic rebellions and Mongol incursions. It was successful at the beginning but ultimately finished with defeat, with most of the army, including the king, captured by Islamic forces.

After he had been released, Louis IX remained in the Holy Land for four years, making what attempts he could towards the re-establishment of the kingdom of Jerusalem. The disharmony between the papacy and Holy Roman Empire incapacitated Europe, with not many answering Louis' calls for help following his capture and ransoming. In 1254, however, Louis was able to return to France having resolved some important agreements. The follow-up of Louis' Crusades was his 1270 expedition to Tunis where he died of dysentery shortly after the campaign landed.

The loss of Jerusalem and defeat at Gaza in 1244 had ultimately marked the collapse of Christian military power in the Holy Land and led to the ascendancy of the Mamluk sultanate. It was in this situation that Louis IX of France and pope Innocent IV initiated the Seventh Crusade to recover Jerusalem.

In the Siege of Jerusalem of the 15th of July 1244, the Holy City Is destroyed. The city's citadel, the Tower of David, surrendered on the 23rd of August 1244, and the Christian population of the city was either driven out or massacred. In 1245, as-Salih captured Damascus, and was awarded the title of sultan by the caliph al-Musta'sim in Baghdad. In 1246, he assessed that his Khwarezmian allies were dangerously uncontrollable, so he turned on them and defeated them near Homs, killing their leaders and dispersing the remnants throughout Syria and Palestine. Three years later when the Crusade began, as-Salih was away fighting his uncle in Syria and quickly returned to Egypt where he died on the 22nd of November 1249.

The treaty signed in 1243 with the Ayyubids did not sustain the peace for long, but the military orders in the kingdom united to fight at Hirbiya in what is often known as the Battle of La Forbie, from the 17th to the

18th of October 1244. Here the Crusaders, led by Walter IV of Brienne, and a Damascus based army met the Egyptian and Khwarezmian armies. In this, which was to be the final major battle between the Frankish fighters and Muslims, five thousand Crusaders died and eight hundred were taken prisoner. Among the slaughtered were Armand de Périgord, Grand Master of the Temple, and Peter II of Sargines, archbishop of Tyre. Christian men taken prisoner included Guillaume de Chateauneuf, Grand Master of the Hospitaller, and the commander Walter IV of Brienne. Only thirty three Templars, twenty seven Hospitallers, and three Teutonic Knights survived, escaping to Ascalon along with Philip of Montfort and Latin patriarch Robert of Nantes.

The first major crisis faced by French king Louis IX was the Saintonge War of 1242 to 1243, pitting Capetian forces supportive of Louis' brother Alphonse of Poitiers against Henry III of England and his continental allies. John II of Soissons supported Louis and would later join his Crusade. Henry hoped to regain Angevin land lost during the reign of his father. The French conclusively defeated the English at the Battle of Taillebourg in July 1242, making it the last major conflict between the two countries until the Anglo-French War in 1778.

The Siege of Jerusalem of 1244 left the Holy City in such a state of ruin that it became virtually unusable for either Christians or Muslims. The sacking of the city and the massacre which accompanied it encouraged Louis IX to organize the first of his Crusades. Even though, the fall of Jerusalem was no longer a crucial event to many European Christians, who knew that the city had passed between Christian and Muslim control numerous times in the two centuries before. This time, despite later calls from the pope, there was no popular enthusiasm for a new crusade. There were too many conflicts within Europe that kept its leaders from embarking on North African adventures.

As 1244 came to an end, Louis was stricken with a severe malarial infection. But, however, while near death he vowed that if he recovered his health that he would set out on a Crusade. He evaded death and when his health allowed him, he took the cross and immediately began preparations for the Crusade.

Innocent IV became pope in June 1243, facing both religious and political crusades since, at that time, the papacy was embroiled in a feud with emperor Frederick II whilst he was excommunicated. Frederick was initially pleased with Innocent's election until it soon became clear that the new pope intended to carry on his predecessor's abstractions. In fear of a scheme to kidnap him, Innocent IV departed from Rome in March 1244 travelling to Lyons and pursued by the emperor's cavalry. He then wrote to Louis and requested asylum but this was guardedly refused.

In exile, the pope presided over First Council of Lyon in 1245 a council which directed a new Crusade under the command of Louis IX with the objective of reconquering the Holy Land.

Innocent IV had inherited from Gregory IX a Crusade targeting the Christian Orthodox Russians. Moreover, he was also the first to seriously face the challenge posed by the Mongol incursion into Europe during 1241. Innocent sent envoys to the Mongols and they also negotiated with Russian princes over Catholic church union with Rome. When the Russians seemed to respond positively, the pope abandoned the scheme of an alliance with the Mongols and aimed instead to form an alliance with the Russians to counter the Mongol threat. In January 1248, Innocent warned the Russians of impending Mongol attacks on Christianity and asked for unity under papal protection in the defence against the invaders and two grand Russian princes accepted the proposal.

Eventually, all eastern European rulers who were not under Mongol domination joined Innocent's alliance even though it was short-lived. In September 1243, Innocent issued the bull Qui iustis causis, authorizing further Northern Crusades.

Innocent IV was, however, determined to keep to

his goal of bringing about the destruction of Frederick II and the attempts undertaken by Louis IX to bring about peace were to no avail. In 1249 the pope ordered a crusade to be preached against Frederick II but the emperor died in December 1250. Innocent, however, continued the struggle against Conrad IV of Germany and his half-brother Manfred of Sicily with unrelenting seriousness. After the death of Conrad IV in May 1254 the pope did recognize the hereditary claims of Conrad's two-year-old son Conradin. Manfred, however, revolted and defeated the papal troops at the Battle of Foggia on the second of December 1254 and Innocent IV died a few days later.

In 1244, the peace of the previous decade was speedily curtailed, neutralising prospects that had appeared better than at any time since the late twelfth century. Most of the Frankish gains in southern Palestine were lost, with Ascalon falling in 1247. This catastrophe in the East put the survival of the Kingdom of Jerusalem into some doubt. Requests for help were dispatched to the West where Louis IX of France had taken the cross after his near-fatal illness. However, it remained unclear whether he had received the cross for its mystical healing properties or as a token of gratitude after his suspension between life and death. The main motive behind the French king's commitment lay involved his personality, piety and ambition. Louis stuck to his decision, repeating his vow and persuading his brothers and those in his court to follow suit.

Louis IX had taken the cross from William of Auvergne, bishop of Paris, without authorization from the pope. In addition to his ecclesiastical role, William was an expert on Middle Eastern affairs and probably had his doubts about the wisdom of the king's decision.

Regardless of various opposition, Louis pressed ahead with the idea that his Crusade was a personal and spiritual rite of passage.

Within the next two months, the pope's edict was issued, with preaching of the Crusade authorized. The cardinal-bishop of Frascati began preaching in France, legitimizing regional preachers and collecting funds. He had been deeply involved in the crusading movement for decades, having personally preached the cross against the Albigensian heretics in 1226, against the Mongols around 1240, and, later, against the Muslims in the Holy Land through Louis' second Crusade.

Recruitment in the French court was not quick to develop. However, Louis' youngest brother Alphonse of Poitiers, took the cross in 1245 and had his army ready in the spring of 1249. Recruitment was concentrated in the kingdom of France, Burgundy, Lorraine and the Low Countries between the Meuse and the Rhine. In 1248, Louis was unsuccessful in convincing

Haakon IV of Norway to join him as commander of the Crusader fleet. Recruits came from across the kingdom, from Flanders and Brittany to Poitou, the Bourbonnais and Languedoc. Early in 1247, Crusaders at Châteaudun had formed a solidarity to purchase materials and ships, providing funding for those who went to fight, and to collect donations.

Henry III of England, defeated by Louis IX in 1242 at Taillebourg, did not want to get involved in a French war but did sign a truce promising not to attack French lands during the Crusade, and a small force of Englishmen, led by William Longespée, also took the cross.

Louis' expenses on the Crusade came to over six times his annual revenues, with the bill for troops running at one thousand livres tournois each day. Louis was largely able to cover this from sources other than his ordinary revenues. Around eighty towns across France raised over seventy thousand livres tournois in 1248.

In October 1245, Louis gathered his barons to receive their agreement and support for the Crusade. The next year, he held another similar gathering in Paris of noblemen to swear loyalty to his children in the event of his non-return from the Crusade. The core of the expedition lay in the ships that Louis had hired, sixteen from Genoa and twenty from Marseille.

The force of ten thousand strong that sailed with

Louis in late August 1248 was of comparable size with that of Richard I of England in April 1191. By the time Louis reached Cyprus, the designated muster point, his agents had spent two years stockpiling vast quantities of foodstuffs.

Louis' preparations had taken three years when extra--ordinary taxes, including on the clergy, were levied to pay for the expedition.

The Seventh Crusade formally began on the 12th of August 1248 when Louis IX departed from Paris with queen Margaret of Provence and her sister Beatrice of Provence. Two of Louis' brothers, Charles I of Anjou, husband of Beatrice, and Robert I of Artois, were also present.

Henry II of England and his mistress Ida de Tosny followed not far behind whilst other English lords had planned to join the Crusade, but Henry had no desire to lose their services at home.

As preparations for the Crusade were finalized, Louis made his progress towards Aigues Mortes, marked as a religious as well as royal procession. The king of France was attempting to assume the leadership of Christendom vacated by the excommunicated emperor. Before leaving Paris for the south, Louis received the insignia of a pilgrim, the Oriflamme from the Abbey of St. Denis. He was conducting his Crusade as king as well as a penitent.

From St. Denis, Louis walked to Notre Dame

dressed as a penitent to hear mass before continuing barefoot to the Abbey of St. Antoine. On his journey south, Louis was garbed as a pilgrim at public appearances. After meeting Innocent IV at Lyons, he travelled towards the Mediterranean, dispensing justice as he went, the first French king to visit the region since his father in 1226. On the 25th of August, Louis sailed to his first destination, Limassol in Cyprus.

Louis IX arrived in Cyprus on the 17th of September 1248 and disembarked the next day accompanied by the queen, her sister, and his chamberlain. After arriving in Cyprus the royal party had a long wait for their forces to assemble since many men were lost to disease. Robert VII of Béthune was among those who died en route to Cyprus. As the troops for the Crusade gathered in Cyprus, they were well received by Henry I of Cyprus.

When the plan of campaign was discussed, it was agreed that Egypt was the objective. It was the richest and most vulnerable province of the Ayyubids and many remembered how the sultan's father al-Kamil had been willing to exchange Jerusalem itself for Damietta in the Fifth Crusade.

Louis wanted to commence operations immediately but was persuaded not to by the grand masters and the Syrian barons. Winter storms were impending and the coast of the Nile delta would then be too dangerous to penetrate. Additionally, they hoped to persuade the king to get involved in internal Ayyubid affairs. The Franks also missed out on an opportunity since the sultan as-Salih Ayyub had taken his army off to fight an-Nasir Yusuf, emir of Aleppo, at Homs. The Templars had by then entered into negotiations with the sultan which suggested that territorial concessions would be met with Frankish intervention. Louis would have no part of such a plan since he had come to fight the heretic Muslims and not to get involved with diplomatic antics. He did, however, order Guillaume de Sonnac to break off negotiations and sent a bunch of demands to the sultan, whose response was equally diplomatic.

Whilst the king refused to negotiate with Muslims, he would, however, with the pagan Mongols following the precedent set by the pope. In December 1248, two Nestorians, named Mark and David, arrived at Nicosia who had been sent by the Mongol general Eljigidei Noyan and brought a letter expressing the Mongols' sympathy for Christianity. Louis responded by sending an Arabic speaker named André de Longjumeau to meet with the general and carried with him various presents. On his arrival at Karakorum, he found that Güyük, with whom the pope had negotiated, had died, with his widow Oghul Qaimish now as regent. She regarded the king's gifts as the tribute due to her but declined anything else. De Longjumeau returned in 1252 with a patronizing letter thanking her vassal

Louis for his attentions, requesting that similar gifts be made each year. Apparently surprised by this response, Louis was still hoping to achieve an eventual Mongol alliance.

Before coming to Cyprus, Louis had people collecting food and weapons for the army on the island, but his providers had not expected to need to feed so many. By Spring-time it was a better period to sail for Egypt and Louis called on local Italian merchants for the necessary ships but many disapproved of his venture and refused to help but by the end of May the ships were provided.

Meanwhile, at Nicosia, Louis received plenty of callers and Hethoum of Armenia sent him gifts. Bohemond V of Antioch requested several hundred archers to protect his principality from brigands, which Louis provided.

Loyalist, Hugh IV of Burgundy, had spent the winter in Achaea and there convinced the ruler William of Villehardouin to join the Crusade and he arrived with ships and Frankish soldiers from the Peloponnese peninsula.

The sultan as-Salih Ayyub had wintered that year in Damascus whilst attempting to finish the conquest of Homs before the Franks invaded. Expecting them to land in Syria, then realizing that their objective was Egypt, the siege was dismantled before he gave orders to his armies to follow him to Cairo. However, he became stricken with tuberculosis and could no longer lead his men personally. He then turned to the aged administrative officer, Fakhr ad-Din ibn as-Shaikh, who had negotiated with Frederick II during the Sixth Crusade, in order for him to command the army. He sent stores of munitions to Damietta and garrisoned them with the Bedouin tribesmen of the Banū Kinana who were known for their courage. He then monitored the coming conflict from his camp at Ashmun al-Rumman, a village to the east of the main branch of the Nile.

During the middle of May 1249, a fleet of one hundred and twenty large boats were put together and the army commencd embarkation. A storm scattered the boats just days into sailing. However, the king finally set sail at the end of May and arrived near Damietta on the 4th of June 1249. Merely a quarter of his combatants came with him, the remainder making their way separately to the Egyptian coast.

Aboard his flagship the Montjoie, Louis' advisers recommended waiting until the rest of the ships arrived before disembarking, but Louis refused their advice. As dawn was breaking on the 5th of June, the Siege of Damietta began. There followed fierce fighting along thesea-line which was led by the king. The onslaught of the knights of France and those of Outremer under John of Ibelin triumphed over the Muslims and at nightfall, Fakhr ad-Din withdrew over a bridge of boats to Damietta. Finding the population there panic-strewn and the garrison hesitant, he made the decision to evacuate the city. All the Muslim civilians fled with him, with the Kinana following, but not before setting fire to the bazaars. Orders to destroy the bridge of boats were not carried out, thus allowing the Crusaders to enter the city where they learned from Christians who had stayed on that Damietta was undefended. The chronicler, Guillaume de Sonnac, wrote of how Damietta had been seized with only one Crusader casualty.

Such a rapid capture of Damietta was not expected but the Nile floods would soon thwart the Crusaders. Louis, knowing of river dangers during the first Battle of Mansurah in 1221 in the Fifth Crusade, decided not to advance until the waters receded. Moreover, he was waiting for the arrival of reinforcements under his brother Alphonse and, meanwhile, Damietta was again transformed into a Frankish city.

The loss of Damietta once again shocked the Muslim world, and, like his father thirty years before, as-Salih Ayyub made the offer to trade Damietta for Jerusalem, an offer which was rejected by Louis saying that he would always refuse to negotiate with an infidel. Meanwhile, those responsible for the loss of the city were punished. Troops were rushed up to Mansurah, a place built by al-Kamil on the site of his victory over the Crusaders of 1221. The terminally ill as-Salih Ayyub was carried there in a litter to organize the army. Bedouins carried out guerrilla tactics around the walls of Damietta, killing any Frank who strayed beyond the walls. The Franks, however, erected dykes and dug ditches to protect the city.

The waters of the Nile waned towards the end of October 1249 and then Alphonse arrived with reinforcements from France. It was therefore time to make the advance on Cairo. Some of the barns of Syria, however, proposed alternatively to launch an attack on Alexandria, surprising the Egyptians and controlling the Mediterranean shore-lines of Egypt. However, Louis' other brother Robert I of Artois opposed such an operation as did the king and on the twentieth of November 1249, the Frankish army struck out from Damietta to go to Mansurah, but leaving a garrison to guard the city where the queen and the patriarch Robert of Nantes were left behind.

King Louis' timing of the move was lucky since As-Salih Ayyub died on the 23rd of November 1249 after having his leg amputated in an attempt to relieve him of a serious abscess. As-Salih's widow, the Armenian-born Shajar al-Durr, temporarily concealed the news of her husband's death but confided in the chief eunuch Jamal ad-Din Mohsen and the commander Fakhr ad-Din. She also forged a document under his signature which appointed Turanshah as heir and Fakhr ad-Din as viceroy.

A Mamluk commander was despatched to bring Turanshah home making his rule rather brief. His mother then married al-Malik al-Muizz Aybak, who served as Mamluk ruler of Egypt, as regent to al-Ashraf Musa and later as sultan. When as-Salih's death eventually got out, the sultana and viceroy were firmly in charge. However the Franks were encouraged by the news and trusted that this Muslim government would shortly collapse.

The route taken by the Crusaders from Damietta was crossed by numerous canals and tributaries of the Nile. Fakhr ad-Din sent his cavalry to harass the Franks as they crossed the canals. There was a battle near Fariskur on the 7th of December 1249, where the Egyptian cavalry was halted and the Templars, against the given orders, pursued those in retreat. On the 14th of December, Louis reached the village of Barāmūn which was merely ten miles to the north of their objective. They then spent the next week encamped on the river banks opposite to Mansurah.

The armies of the Europeans and Egypt faced each other on opposite sides of the canal for six weeks. This culminated in a second Battle of Mansurah that wound up on the 11th of February 1250, the Crusaders having won.

The Egyptians had attempted to attack the Franks

to the rear but this was stopped by Charles I of Anjou. Louis had ordered construction work to bridge the waterway but enemy bombardment, including Greek fire, caused this to be abandoned. At one point, an Egyptian Coptic group came to the camp and offered to reveal where a ford across the canal could be found. As dawn was breaking on the 8th of February, the Crusaders set off across the ford with the king leading the advancing army. Hugh IV of Burgundy and Renaud de Vichiers stayed behind to guard the camp. The advance guard was led by Robert I of Artois and supported by the Templars and an English contingent but he was under orders not to attack until directed by the king. However, once Robert and his fighters had crossed the river he feared that the element of surprise would be gone unless he took the offensive. Robert's men attacked the Egyptian camp whilst the Egyptians were unprepared and still beginning their day. The Muslims were slaughtered while searching for their weapons and the survivors fled to Mansurah. Fakhr ad-Din had just heard the noise of the attack and leapt onto his horse to ride into the battle but was was cut down by Templar knights.

Following the taking of the Egyptian camp, Robert's commanders again cautioned him to wait for their main army to arrive but Robert called the Templars and the English cowards and charged after the fleeing Egyptians.

Although Fakhr ad-Din was dead, his commander Rukn ad-Din Baibars, who was later a Mamluk sultan, restored order amongst the Egyptians. Strategically situating fighters in the town, he allowed the Frankish cavalry through the open gate and the Egyptians attacked them from the side streets. The horses, unable to turn in the narrow spaces, were thrown into confusion. A few knights who escaped on foot to the river got drowned in its waters. The Templars fell fighting, with less than two percent surviving who hurried off to warn the king.

When he heard of the battle at the Egyptian camp, Louis drew up his own front line ready to meet an attack, and sent his engineers to build a bridge over the stream. The cross-bow-men had been left on the far side to guard the crossing, and after needed to be brought over on a pontoon which neared completion. At this point the Mamluks speedily charged out of the town towards the king's lines. Keeping his force in reserve while the enemy poured arrows into their ranks, Louis ordered a counterattack as soon as the enemy's ammunition ran short. The cavalries of the opposing sides fought back and forth with one attempting to hinder the building of the pontoon. The pontoon, however, was quickly finished and the cross-bow-men crossed over then the Egyptians retreated back into the city. Louis had gained a victory but at the cost of the loss of much of his force and their commanders, including his younger brother. However, the victory was short-lived.

Louis found himself in a situation reminiscent of that of during the Fifth Crusade when the Crusader army that had captured Damietta was eventually forced to retreat and he realised that he would likely suffer a similar fate unless the Egyptians could be persuaded to offer acceptable terms. On the eleventh of February 1250, the Egyptians renewed their attack, supported by reinforcements from the south and engaged the Franks in battle.

Charles I of Anjou and the Syrian and Cypriot barons at the left held their ground, but the remnants of the Templars and the French nobles at the right wavered and had to be rescued by the king. Templar master Guillaume de Sonnac, who had already lost an eye, lost the other and died from it. Acting Hospitaller master Jean de Ronay was also killed. At nightfall, the Muslims gave up the assault and returned to the town.

For eight weeks Louis waited at the Crusader camp in hope that the leadership problem in Cairo would work to his advantage. But instead, on the 28th of February 1250, Turanshah arrived from Damascus where he had been proclaimed sultan following his father's death and his arrival was the thrust for a new Egyptian offensive. A small fleet of light boats were made and transported by camel to the lower portion of the Nile where they were used to intercept the boats that brought food from Damietta. They then captured more than eighty Frankish ships. In mid March 1250 alone, a convoy of thirty-two boats were lost and the Franks were also ravaged by famine and disease.

The Battle of Fariskur fought on the 6th of April 1250 was the decisive defeat of Louis' army. Louis knew that the army should be moved to Damietta and negotiations begun, offering Turanshah the exchange of Damietta for Jerusalem. The Egyptians recognised his poor position and rejected the offer when made. In planning their retreat, Louis' officers urged the king to go immediately to Damietta but he refused to leave his men. It was decided that the sick should be sent by boat down the Nile and the able-bodied men should march back along the road by which they had arrived. They departed early on the 5th of April and a pain-wracked journey began, with the king at the rear and the Egyptians in pursuit. The Franks did manage to get across the al-Bahr as-Saghit but neglected to destroy the pontoon behind them and the Egyptian forces crossed over and began attacking the Franks from all sides. Their attacks, however, were repulsed and the Franks moved slowly on but Louis fekl ill that night. The following day, the Muslims surrounded the crusaders at the town of Fariskur, ten miles southwest of Damietta, and attacked them in full force.

To the sick and weary soldiers it was obvious that the end was near and Geoffrey of Sergines, commander of the royal bodyguard, sheltered the king at nearby Sharamsah. It was on the 6th of April that Louis' surrender was negotiated directly with the sultan by Philip of Montfort. The king and his entourage were taken in chains to Mansurah where his whole army was rounded up and led into captivity whilst the ships conveying the sick to Damietta were surrounded and also captured making the Egyptian victory absolute.

The Egyptians themselves were surprised by the large number of prisoners taken, estimated by the sultan to be thirty thousand, likely most of Louis' force. The Egyptians, unable to guard all the prisoners, executed the infirm immediately and each day several hundred more were decapitated, by order of the sultan. Louis, however, was moved to a private residence in Mansurah and the Crusader leaders were kept together in a larger prison. While they were threatened with death, their value for ransom allowed them to stay alive. Jean de Joinville, onboard one of the captured ships, saved his life by claiming to be the king's cousin. It was later revealed that he was actually the emperor's cousin, which served him well since the prestige of Frederick II among the Egyptians was a bonus.

When Louis was asked by the sultan to surrender

not only Damietta but all the Frankish lands in Syria, Louis stated that they were not under his control, but rather that of Conrad II of Jerusalem, the emperor's son, thus the demand was soon dropped.

The final terms exacted from Louis, however, were rather harsh. He was to ransom himself by the surrender of Damietta and his army by the payment of a million bezants. After the terms were agreed to, the king and the barons were taken down the river to Fariskur, where the sultan had taken residence. From there they were to go on to Damietta, the city to be handed over on the 30th of April 1250.

The possibility of the bargain was in part due to the queen. At the time that Louis had commenced his march on Mansurah, Margaret of Provence was in advanced stages of pregnancy. Their son John Tristan was born on the 8th of April, three days after the news came of the surrender of the army at the same time as she found out that the Pisans and Genoese were planning to evacuate Damietta due to lack of food. She understood that Damietta could not withhold the onslaught without assistance from the Italians and she henceforth requested help from their leaders.

Should Damietta be abandoned there would be nothing to offer towards the release of her husband. She proposed buying all the food in the city and distributing it around causing them to agree to stay and

, hence, boosting the morale of the city. Soon after that, she was taken to Acre, and the Latin patriarch, Robert of Nantes, went on to complete arrangements for a ransom with the sultan.

Robert arrived to find Turanshah dead, murdered on the 2nd of May 1250 in a coup prompted by his stepmother, Shajar al-Durr and led by Baibars. Aybak was elevated to become commander after Turanshah's assassination and later married his widow. Some Mamluks brandished their swords before the king and the captive barons, still covered with the executed sultan's blood, but, eventually the Egyptians authorized the agreed-upon terms.

When Louis was asked to swear that he would renounce Jesus Christ if he reneged in his bargain, he made a refusal. On the 6th of May, Geoffrey of Sergines transferred Damietta over to the Muslim vanguard. The king and the nobles were later brought there and Louis set about locating funds for the initial instalment of the ransom. At first he was unable to find enough and until the balance could be found, the Egyptians stalled on releasing Alphonse , the king's brother. The Templars, known to have plentiful funds, eventually agreed to provide what was needed.

Louis and the barons set sail for Acre, where they arrived after a stormy voyage on the 12th of May, having left behind many wounded soldiers at Damietta and, contrary to their promises, the Muslims massacred all of them.

The Seventh Crusade did not end for another four years. However, there were no further battles. In Acre, Louis pursued the release of his imprisoned army and was the last of the Crusader leaders to actually reach the shores of the eastern Mediterranean. When the extent of the disaster reached mainland Europe, unrest in Venice and other Italian cities was reported and France indulged in public mourning.

The death of Turanshah effectively ended the Ayyubid dynasty begun by Saladin. The Bahri Mamluks who essentially controlled Egypt at that time installed as sultan the six-year-old al-Ashraf Musa. The actual power in Egypt was still, however, exercised by Aybak, who had returned to his position of atabeg and Egypt would remain a Mamluk sultanate on through to 1517.

On the 13th of December 1250, Frederick II, who had remained respected in Muslim circles, died in Italy.

THE FRENCH WARS OF RELIGION

The French Wars of Religion were a period of civil war from 1562 to 1598 which was between Catholics and Huguenots. There have been estimates made that between two and four million people died from the violence, or from famine or diseases which were exacerbated by the conflict.

When the fighting ended in 1598, Henry of Navarre, who had converted to Catholicism in 1593, was proclaimed Henry IV of France and issued the Edict of Nantes, which granted substantial rights and freedoms to the Huguenots. Catholics, however, continued to have a hostile attitude towards Protestants in general and of Henry. His assassination in 1610 catalysed a fresh episode of Huguenot rebellions in the 1620s.

Tensions between people of the two religions had been getting stronger since the 1530's which exacerbated the existing regional divisions. The death of Henry II of France in July 1559 began a protracted struggle for power between his widow, Catherine de' Medici, and other powerful noble people.. Moderates, also known as Politiques, tried to maintain order by centralising power and making concessions to Huguenots, rather than the policies of repression pursued by Henry II and his father Francis I. They were supported by Catherine de' Medici in the beginning but her January 1562 Edict of Saint-Germain was strongly opposed by the Guise faction and led to an outbreak of widespread fighting that March. She later hardened her stance and backed the 1572 St. Bartholomew's Day massacre in Paris, an outrage which resulted in Catholic mobs killing between five and thirty thousand Protestants throughout France.

The wars threatened the authority of the monarchy and the kings of the House of Valois. Their Bourbon successor Henry IV responded by creating a strong central state and encouraging toleration of Huguenots. The latter policy was sustained until 1685, when Henry's grandson, Louis XIV of France, revoked the Edict of Nantes.

THE IRAN IRAQ WAR

The war between Iran and Iraq was a military conflict that lasted from September 1980 until August 1988. It began when Iraq's forces invaded Iran and lasted for almost eight years, until the acceptance by both sides of the United Nations Security Council Resolution 598. Iraq's main reasoning behind the attack against Iran was cited as the need to prevent Ruhollah Khomeini, who had spearheaded Iran's Islamic Revolution in 1979, from exporting the stronger Islamic ideology to Iraq. There were also substantial fears among the Iraqi leadership of Saddam Hussein that Iran, a theocratic state with a population composed predominantly of Shia Muslims, as Iran was, would exploit sectarian tensions in Iraq by rallying Iraq's Shia majority against Saddam's Ba'athist government, which was officially secular and dominated by Sunni Muslims.

Iraq's leadership also wanted to replace Iran as the principle power player in the Persian Gulf, which was not seen as an achievable objective prior to the Islamic Revolution because of Iran's economic and military superiority as well as its close relationships with the United States and Israel.

The 1980 War culminated from a long-running history of territorial border disputes between the two countries. It was thought that the Iraquis planned to retake the eastern bank of the Shatt al-Arab, the confluence of the Euphrates and Tigris rivers that it had ceded to Iran in the 1975 Algiers Agreement.

Following the outbreak of hostilities, Iraqi support for Arab separatists inside of Iran increased. Moreover, at this time, claims arose proclaiming suspicion that Iraq was seeking to annex Iran's Khuzestan province. However, Saddam Hussein publicly stated in November 1980 that Iraq was not seeking an annexation of any Iranian territory but it is believed that Saddam had sought to establish sovereignty over Khuzestan, a province of southwestern Iran which borders on Iraq.

It is thought that the Iraqi leadership had hoped to take advantage of Iran's post-revolutionary pandemonium and expected a conclusive victory over a badly weakened Iran. However, the Iraqi military only made progress for three months and by December 1980, their invasion had halted and the Iranians began to gain success against the Iraqis and, by June 1982, had regained almost all lost territory.

After they had driven Iraqi forces back to the prewar border lines, the Iranians rejected United Nations Security Council Resolution 514 and launched a counter-invasion of Iraq, an offensive within Iraqi territory lasting for five years. w Iraq, however, took back the initiative in the middle of 1988 and consequently launched a series of major new offensives, but which finally led to the conclusion of the war being at a stalemate situation.The eight years of war-exhaustion and economic devastation all influenced Iran's acceptance of a ceasefire brokered by the United Nations Security Council. In total, around half a million people were killed during that war. In Iran, the war is known as the Imposed War and the Holy Defense.

When Iraq launched their full-scale invasion of Iran in September 1980, the Iraqi Air Force made surprise air strikes on ten Iranian airfields with the objective of destroying the Iranian Air Force. The attack damaged some of Iran's airbase infrastructure but failed to destroy a significant number of aircraft. The Iraqi Air Force was only able to strike in depth with a few MiG-23BN, Tu-22, and Su-20 aircraft, but Iran had built reinforced aircraft shelters where most of its combat aircraft were stored.

The following day, the Iraquis made a ground invasion along a battle front of six hundred and forty-four kilometres. They made three simultaneous attacks.

Saddam had hoped that an attack on Iran would cause such a blow to Komeini's prestige that it would lead to the new government's downfall, or minimally, silence calls for Saddam's overthrow.

Of Iraq's six divisions that invaded by ground, four were sent over the border into the Iranian province of Khuzestan to cut off the Shatt al-Arab river from the rest of Iran and to establish a territorial security zone. The other two divisions invaded across the northern and central part of the Iraqi/Iranian border to prevent an Iranian counter-attack.

The two armoured divisions secured the territory bounded by the cities of Khorramshahr, Ahvaz, Susangerd, and Musian. On the central front, the Iraqis occupied Mehran, advanced towards the foothills of the Zagros Mountains, and were able to block the traditional Tehran–Baghdad invasion route by securing territory forward of Qasr-e Shirin, Iran. On the northern part of the front, the Iraqis tried to establish a strong defensive position opposite Suleimaniya to protect their Kirkuk oil complex.

Iraqi hopes of an uprising by the ethnic Arabs of Khuzestan fell short of materialising, in part since the majority of the ethnic Arabs remained loyal to Iran. Even though the Iraqi air invasion surprised the Iranians, the Iranian air force retaliated the following day with a large-scale attack against Iraqi air bases and infrastructure in Operation Kaman 99. Groups of F-4 Phantom and F-5 Tiger fighter jets attacked targets throughout Iraq, including oil facilities, dams, petrochemical plants, oil refineries and Mosul Airbase.

The Iraqis were taken by surprise by the power of the assaults, which caused them heavy losses and economic disruption. The Iranians, however, received heavy losses also, losing many aircraft and aircrews to Iraqi air defences.

Iranian Army Aviation's AH-1 Cobra helicopter gunships began attacks on the advancing Iraqi divisions, along with F-4 Phantoms armed with AGM-65 Maverick missiles. They destroyed numerous armoured vehicles and impeded the Iraqi advance, though not completely stopping it. At the same time, Iraqi air attacks on Iran were repelled by Iran's F-14A Tomcat interceptor fighter jets, using AIM-54A Phoenix missiles. These brought down a dozen of Iraq's Soviet-built fighters in the first two days of battle.

The Iranian military, police force and Revolutionary Guards all conducted their operations separately which resulted in the Iraqi invading forces not having to face coordinated resistance.

On the 24th of September, the Iranian Navy attacked Basra, in Iraq, and destroyed two oil terminals near the Iraqi port Al-Faw; this reduced Iraq's ability to export oil. On the 30th of September, Iran's air force launched Operation Scorch Sword, striking and badly damaging the Osirak Nuclear Reactor near Baghdad, which was only just nearing completion. By the beginning of October, Baghdad had been subjected to eight air attacks and in response, Iraq launched aerial strikes against Iranian targets.

The mountainous border between Iran and Iraq made major ground level invasion impossibly difficult, therefore, air strikes were used instead. The Iraqi invasion's first waves were a series of air strikes targeted at Iranian airfields and they also attempted to bomb Tehran, Iran's capital and command centre, into submission.

On the 22nd of September, a prolonged battle began in the Iranian city of Khorramshahr, eventually leaving about seven thousand killed on both sides, inspiring the Iranians to call Khorramshahr "City of Blood".

An estimated two hundred thousand fresh Iranian troops arrived at the front by November, many of them ideologically committed volunteers.

Although Khorramshahr was eventually captured, the battle had delayed the Iraqis enough to allow the large-scale deployment of the Iranian military. In November, Saddam ordered his forces to advance towards Dezful and Ahvaz, and lay sieges to both cities. However, the Iraqi offensive was put back by Iranian militias and air power. Iran's air force had destroyed Iraq's army supply depots and fuel supplies, and was strangling the country through an aerial siege but Iran's supplies had not been exhausted, despite sanctions.

On the 28th of November, Iran launched Operation Morvarid, a combined air and sea attack which destroyed eighty percent of Iraq's navy and all of its radar sites in the southern portion of the country. When Iraq laid siege to Abadan and dug its troops in around the city, it was unable to blockade the port, which allowed Iran to resupply Abadan by sea.

But by now, Iraq's strategic reserves had been depleted, and it lacked the power to go on any major offensives until late on in the war. On the 7th of December, Saddam announced that Iraq was going on the defensive. However, by the end of 1980, Iraq had destroyed about five hundred Western-built Iranian tanks and had captured one hundred others.

For the next eight months, both sides were on a defensive footing, with the exception of the Battle of Dezful. The Iranians needed more time to reorganise their forces after the setbacks inflicted in 1979 and 1980. Iraq had mobilised twenty-one divisions for the invasion, while Iran countered with only thirteen regular army divisions and one brigade. Of the regular divisions, only seven were deployed to the border.

The war descended into World War One style trench warfare but with tanks and modern late-twentieth century weapons. Due to the power of Iranian held anti-tank weapons such as the RPG-7, armored manoeuvre by the Iraqis was very costly, and, consequently, their tanks became entrenched into static positions.

Whilst Iraq began firing Scud missiles into Dezful and Ahvaz, and used terror bombing to bring the war to the Iranian civilian population, Iran launched dozens of human wave assaults by its soldiers.

By the 5th of January 1981, Iran had reorganised its forces enough to launch a large-scale offensive which was called Operation Nasr and they launched their major armoured offensive from Dezful. However, the Iranian tanks raced through Iraqi lines with their flanks unprotected and with no infantry support. As a result, they were cut off by Iraqi tanks. In the ensuing Battle of Dezful, the Iranian armoured divisions were almost wiped out in one of the biggest tank battles of the war. When the Iranian tanks tried to manoeuvre, they became stuck in the mud of the marshes, resulting in many tanks being abandoned. The Iraqis lost forty five T-55 and T-62 tanks, while the Iranians lost one or two hundred Chieftain and M-60 tanks. Newa reporters counted approximately one hundred and fifty destroyed or deserted Iranian tanks, plus forty Iraqi tanks.

The Islamic Republic government in Iran was further distracted by internal fighting between the regime and the Mujahedin e-Khalq (MEK) on the streets of Iran's major cities in June 1981 and again in September. In 1983, the MEK started an alliance with Iraq following a meeting between MEK leader Massoud Rajavi and Iraqi Deputy Prime minister Tariq Aziz.

The surprise attack on H-3 airbase is considered to be one of the most sophisticated air operations of the war. The Iraqi Air Force, badly damaged by the Iranians, was moved to the H-3 Airbase in Western Iraq, near the Jordanian border and away from Iran. However, on the 3rd of April 1981, the Iranian air force used eight F-4 Phantom fighter bombers, four F-14 Tomcats, three Boeing 707 refuelling tankers, and one Boeing 747 command plane to launch a surprise attack on H3, destroying many Iraqi fighter jets and bombers.

Despite their successful H-3 airbase attack and in addition to other air attacks, the Iranian Air Force was made to cancel its successful one hundred and eighty day air offensive and, in addition, they abandoned their attempted control of Iranian airspace. They had been seriously weakened by sanctions and pre-war purges and the Iranian Air Force could not survive further attrition. They then decided to limit their losses, abandoning efforts to control Iranian airspace and would henceforth fight on the defensive, trying to deter the Iraqis rather than engaging them.

While throughout 1981 and 1982 the Iraqi air force would remain weak, within the next few years they would rearm and expand again, and begin to regain the strategic initiative.

The human wave attacks, while extremely bloody as tens of thousands of troops died in the process, when used in combination with infiltration and surprise, caused major Iraqi defeats. As the Iraqis would dig in their tanks and infantry into static, entrenched positions, the Iranians would manage to break through the lines and encircle entire divisions.

After the Iraqi offensive stalled in March 1981, there was little change in the front other than Iran retaking the high ground above Susangerd in May. By late 1981, Iran returned to the offensive and launched a new operation, Operation Samen-ol-A'emeh, ending the Iraqi Siege of Abadan on the 27th to 29th of September 1981. The Iranians used a combined force of regular army artillery with small groups of armour, supported by infantry. On the 15th of October, after breaking the siege, a large Iranian convoy was ambushed by Iraqi tanks, and during the ensuing tank battle Iran lost twenty Chieftains and other armoured vehicles and withdrew from the previously gained territory.

On the 29th of November 1981, Iran began Operation Tariq al-Qods with three army brigades and seven Revolutionary Guard brigades. The Iraqis failed to properly patrol their occupied areas, and the Iranians constructed a fourteen kilometre long road through the unguarded sand dunes, then launched their attack from behind Iraqi troops. The town of

Bostan was retaken from Iraqi divisions by the 7th of December. By this time the Iraqi Army was experiencing serious morale problems, compounded by the fact that Operation Tariq al-Qods marked the first use of Iranian "human wave" tactics, where the Revolutionary Guard light infantry repeatedly charged at Iraqi positions, oftentimes without the support of armour or air power. The fall of Bostan exacerbated the Iraqis' logistical problems, forcing them to use a roundabout route from Ahvaz to the south to re-supply their troops. Six thousand Iranians and over two thousand Iraqis were killed in the operation.

On the 19th of March, the Iraqis, who realised that the Iranians were planning to attack, decided to pre-empt them with Operation al-Fawz al-'Azim and using many tanks, helicopters, and fighter jets, they attacked the Iranian build-up around the Roghabiyeh pass. Though Saddam and his generals thought they had succeeded, the Iranian forces had actually remained almost fully operational. The Iranians had built up concentrated forces by bringing fighters directly from the cities and towns throughout Iran in trains, buses, and private cars and, as a result, Saddam's army was unprepared for the Iranian offensives to come.

Iran's next major offensive was called Operation Undeniable Victory. On the 22nd of March 1982, Iran launched a surprise attack on the Iraqi forces using Chinook helicopters. They landed behind Iraqi lines, silenced their artillery, and captured an Iraqi head-quarters. The Iranian Basij then launched "human wave" attacks, consisting of one thousand fighters per wave and although they sustained heavy losses, they eventually broke through Iraqi lines.

The Revolutionary Guard and regular army followed up by surrounding the Iraqi 9th and 10th Armoured and 1st Mechanised Divisions that had camped close to the Iranian town of Shush. The Iraqis launched a counter-attack using their 12th Armoured division to break the encirclement and rescue the surrounded divisions. Iraqi tanks came under attack by ninety-five Iranian F-4 Phantom and F-5 Tiger fighter jets which destroyed much of the division.

Operation Undeniable Victory was an Iranian victory and Iraqi forces were driven away from Shush, Dezful and Ahvaz. The Iranian armed forces destroyed nearly four hundred Iraqi tanks and armored vehicles but not without cost since, in just the first day of the battle, the they lost a little under two hundred tanks themselves.

Next, in preparation for Operation Beit ol-Moqad-das, the Iranians launched numerous air raids against Iraq air bases, destroying forty-seven jets, including Iraq's brand new Mirage F-1 fighter jets from France. This provided Iranian air superiority over the battlefield while also allowing monitoring of Iraqi troop movements.

On the 29th of April, Iran launched their offensive when seventy thousand Revolutionary Guard and Basij members struck on several places; Bostan, Susangerd, the west bank of the Karun River, and Ahvaz. The Basij launched human wave attacks, which were followed up by the regular army and Revolutionary Guard support along with tanks and helicopters and under this heavy pressure, the Iraqi forces retreated. Then, by the 12th of May, Iran had driven out all Iraqi forces from the Susangerd area. .

The Iraqis retreated to the Karun River, with only Khorramshahr and a few outlying areas remaining in their control, then, Saddam ordered seventy thousand troops to be placed around the city of Khorramshahr. Saddam Hussein even visited Khorramshahr in a dramatic gesture, swearing that the city would never be surrendered. However, Khorramshahr's only resupply point was across the Shatt al-Arab river and the Iranian air force began bombing the supply bridges to the city, while their artillery focused on the besieged garrison.

However, in the early morning hours of the 23rd of May 1982, the Iranians began the drive towards Khorramshahr across the Karun River. This part of Operation Beit ol-Moqaddas was spear-headed by the 77th Khorasan division with tanks along with the Revolutionary Guard and Basij. The Iranians hit the Iraqis with destructive air strikes and massive artillery barrages, crossed the Karun River, captured bridgeheads, and launched human wave attacks towards the city. Saddam's defensive barricade collapsed and in less than forty-eight hours of fighting, the city fell and nineteen thousand Iraqis surrendered to the Iranians. A total of ten thousand Iraqis were killed or wounded in Khorramshahr, while the Iranians suffered thirty thousand casualties.

The fighting severely knocked back the size of the Iraqi military: its strength fell from two hundred and ten to one hundred and fifty thousand troops; over twenty thousand Iraqi soldiers were killed and over thirty thousand captured; two out of four active armoured divisions and at least three mechanised divisions fell to less than a brigade's strength. The Iranians had captured over four hundred and fifty tanks and armoured personnel carriers.

The Iraqi Air Force also found itself severely depleted. After losing aproximately fifty five aircraft since early December 1981, it had only one hundred intact fighter-bombers and interceptors left. A defector who flew to Syria in June 1982 revealed that the Iraqi Air Force had only three squadrons of fighter-bombers capable of mounting operations into Iran.

At this time, Saddam believed that his army was too demoralised and damaged to hold onto Khuzestan and other swathes of Iranian territory. He withdrew his remaining forces, redeploying them in defence along the border instead. However, his troops continued to occupy some key Iranian border areas of Iran, including the disputed territories that prompted his invasion, notably the Shatt al-Arab waterway.

In response to failures against the Iranians in Khorramshahr, Saddam ordered the executions of several of his Generals and Colonels and at least a dozen other high-ranking officers were also executed during this time.

In April 1982, the rival Ba'athist regime in Syria, one of the few nations that supported Iran, closed the Kirkuk–Baniyas pipeline that had allowed Iraqi oil to reach tankers on the Mediterranean, reducing the Iraqi budget by five billion dollars per month. Syria's closure of the Kirkuk–Baniyas pipeline left Iraq with the pipeline to Turkey as the only means of exporting oil, along with transporting oil by tanker truck to the port of Aqaba in Jordan.However, the Turkish pipeline had a capacity of only half a million barrels per day, which was insufficient to pay for the war. However, Saudi Arabia, Kuwait, and the other Gulf states saved Iraq from bankruptcy by providing it with an average of sixty billion dollars in subsidies per year. Even though Iraq had previously been hostile towards other Gulf states, the threat of Iranian fundamentalism was seen as more of a threat. They were especially inclined to fear Iranian victory after Ayatollah Khomeini declared monarchies to be illegitimate and an un-Islamic form of government. Khomeini's statement was widely seen as a call to overthrow the Gulf monarchies.

Iraq began receiving support from the United States and west European countries as well. It was given diplomatic, monetary, and military support by the United States, including massive loans and intelligence on Iranian deployments gathered by American spy satellites. The Iraqis relied heavily on American satellite footage and radar planes to detect Iranian troop movements, and this enabled Iraq to move troops to the site before a battle.

With Iranian success on the battlefield, the United States increased its support of Saddam's government, supplying intelligence, economic aid, and dual-use equipment and vehicles, as well as normalizing its inter-governmental relations. President Ronald Reagan decided that the United States "could not afford to allow Iraq to lose the war to Iran", and that the United States "would do whatever was necessary to prevent Iraq from losing".

In 1982, American President Reagan removed Iraq from the list of countries "supporting terrorism".At the same time, the Soviet Union, angered with Iran for purging and destroying the communist Tudeh Party, sent large shipments of weapons to Iraq. The Iraqi Air Force was replenished with Soviet,

Chinese, and French fighter jets and attack/transport helicopters. Iraq also replenished their stocks of small arms and anti-tank weapons such as AK-47s and rocket-propelled grenades from its supporters. The depleted tank forces were replenished with more Soviet and Chinese tanks, and the Iraqis were reinvigorated in the face of the coming Iranian onslaught.

Iran did not have the money to purchase arms to the same extent as Iraq did. They counted on China, North Korea, Libya, Syria, and Japan for supplying anything from weapons and munitions to logistical and engineering equipment.

On the 20th of June 1982, Saddam announced that he wanted to sue for peace and proposed an immediate ceasefire and withdrawal from Iranian territory within two weeks. Khomeini responded by saying the war would not end until a new government was installed in Iraq and reparations paid. He proclaimed that Iran would invade Iraq and would not stop until the Ba'ath regime was replaced by an Islamic republic. Iran supported a government in exile for Iraq, the Supreme Council of the Islamic Revolution in Iraq, led by exiled Iraqi cleric Mohammad Baqer al-Hakim, which was dedicated to over-throwing the Ba'ath party.

The decision to invade Iraq was taken after much debate within the Iranian government. One faction, wanted to accept the ceasefire, as most of Iranian soil had been recaptured. In particular, General Shirazi and Zahirnejad were both opposed to the invasion of Iraq on logistical grounds, and stated they would consider resigning if "unqualified people continued to meddle with the conduct of the war". The Iranians also hoped that its attacks would ignite a revolt against Saddam's rule by the Shia and Kurdish population of Iraq, and hopefully resulting in his downfall.

At a cabinet meeting in Baghdad, a Minister of Health suggested that Saddam could step down temporarily as a way of easing Iran towards a ceasefire, and then afterwards would come back to power.

By and large, Iraq remained on the defensive for the next five years, unable or unwilling to launch any major offensives, while Iran launched more than seventy offensives. Iraq's strategy changed from holding territory in Iran to denying Iran any major gains in Iraq, as well as holding onto disputed territories along the border.

By 1988, Iraq was spending between forty and seventy-five percent of its GDP on military equipment and Saddam had also more than doubled the size of the Iraqi army, from two hundred thousand to half a million soldiers. Iraq also began launching air raids against Iranian border cities. The Combat Engineer Corps built bridges across water obstacles, laid minefields, erected earthen revetments, dug trenches, built machine gun nests, and prepared new defence lines and fortifications.

Iraq was focussing on using in-depth defence to defeat the Iranians and created multiple static defence lines. When faced with large-scale Iranian attack, where human waves would overrun it's forward entrenched infantry defences, the Iraqis would often retreat, but their static defences would bleed the Iranians and channel them into certain directions, drawing them into traps or pockets. Iraqi air and artillery attacks would then pin the Iranians down, while tanks and mechanised infantry attacks using mobile warfare would push them back. While Iranian human wave attacks were successful against the dug-in Iraqi forces in Khuzestan, they had trouble breaking through Iraq's defence in depth lines. Iraq had a logistical advantage in their defence: the front was located near the main Iraqi bases and arms depots, allowing their army to be efficiently supplied. By contrast, the front in Iran was a considerable distance away from the main Iranian bases and arms depots, and as such, Iranian troops and supplies had to travel through mountain ranges before arriving at the front.

The Iranian generals wanted to launch an all-out attack on Baghdad and seize it before the weapon shortages continued to manifest further. Instead, that was rejected as being unfeasible, and the decision was made to capture one area of Iraq after the other in the hopes that a series of blows delivered foremost by the Revolutionary Guards Corps would force a political solution to the war, including Iraq withdrawing completely from the disputed territories along the border.

The Iranians planned their next attack in southern Iraq, near Basra. Called Operation Ramadan, it involved over one hundred and eighty thousand troops from both sides, and was one of the largest land battles since World War II. Iranian strategy dictated that they launch their primary attack on the weakest point of the Iraqi lines.

However, the Iraqis found out about Iran's battle plans and moved all of their forces to the area the Iranians planned to attack. The Iraqis were equipped with tear gas to use against the enemy, which would be the first major use of chemical warfare during the conflict, driving an entire attack division to chaos.

Over one hundred thousand Revolutionary Guards and Basij volunteer forces charged towards the Iraqi lines. The Iraqi troops had entrenched themselves in formidable defenses, and had set up a network of bunkers and artillery positions. The Basij used human waves, and were even used to clear the Iraqi minefields, allowing the Revolutionary Guards to advance. Combatants came so close to one another that Iranians were able to board Iraqi tanks and throw grenades inside the hulls. By the eighth day, the Iranians had gained sixteen kilometres inside Iraq and had captured several causeways.

On the 16th of July, the Iranians tried again further north and managed to push the Iraqis back. However, only thirteen kilometres from Basra, the poorly equipped Iranian forces were surrounded on three sides by Iraqis with heavy weaponry and some were captured, while many were killed. Only a last-minute attack by Iranian AH-1 Cobra helicopters stopped the Iraqis from routing the Iranians. Three more similar attacks occurred around the Khorramshahr-Baghdad road area towards the end of the month, but none were significantly successful. Iraq had concentrated three armoured divisions, the 3rd, 9th, and 10th, as a counter-attack force to attack any penetrations. They were successful in defeating the Iranian breakthroughs, even though they suffered heavy losses. The total casualty toll had grown to include eighty thousand soldiers and civilians. Four hundred Iranian tanks and armoured vehicles were destroyed or abandoned, while Iraq lost no fewer than three hundred and seventy tanks.

After Iran's failure in Operation Ramadan, they carried out only a few smaller attacks; they launched two limited offensives aimed at reclaiming the Sumar Hills and isolating the Iraqi pocket at Naft shahr at the international border, both of which were part of the disputed territories still under Iraqi occupation, after which they aimed to capture the Iraqi border town of Mandali. They then planned to take the Iraqis by surprise using Basij militiamen, army helicopters, and some armoured forces, then stretch their defences and to open a road to Baghdad for future exploitation. During Operation Muslim ibn Aqil, Iran recovered one hundred and fifty square kilometres of disputed territory straddling the international border and reached the outskirts of Mandali before being stopped by Iraqi helicopter and armoured vehicle attacks.

During Operation Muharram, on the 1st to the 21st of November, the Iranians captured part of the Bayat oilfield using partly their fighter jets and helicopters, destroying one hundred and five Iraqi tanks, 70 APCs, and seven planes with few losses. They nearly breached the Iraqi lines but failed to capture Mandali after the Iraqis sent reinforcements, including brand new T-72 tanks, which possessed armour that could not be pierced from the front by Iranian TOW missiles. The Iranian advance was also impeded by heavy rains. Three and a half thousand Iraqis and an unknown number of Iranians died, with only minor gains for Iran.

After the failure of the 1982 summer offensives, the Iranians believed that a major effort along the entire breadth of the front would yield victory. During the course of 1983, they launched five major assaults along the front, though none achieved substantial success, even though they staged even more massive "human wave" attacks.

By this time, it was estimated that no more than seventy Iranian fighter aircraft remained operational at any one time.Iranian fighter pilots had superior training compared to their Iraqi counterparts, since most had received training from US officers before the 1979 revolution, and would continue to dominate in combat. However, aircraft shortages, the size of defended territory/airspace, and American intelligence supplied to Iraq allowed the Iraqis to exploit gaps in Iranian airspace. Iraqi air campaigns met little opposition, striking over half of Iran, as the Iraqis were able to gain air superiority towards the end of the war.In Operation Before the Dawn, launched on the 6th of February 1983, the Iranians employed two hundred thousand "last reserve" Revolutionary Guard troops. They attacked along a forty kilometre stretch near al-Amarah, Iraq, about two hundred kilometres southeast of Baghdad, in an attempt to reach the highways connecting northern and southern Iraq. This attack, however, was stalled by sixty kilometres of hilly escarpments, forests, and river torrents blanketing the way to al-Amarah,. The Iraqis could not force the Iranians back.

Iran directed artillery on Basra, Al Amarah, and Mandali but suffered a large number of casualties clearing minefields and breaching Iraqi anti-tank mines, which Iraqi engineers were unable to replace. After this battle, Iran reduced its use of human wave attacks, though they still remained a key tactic as the war went on.

In April 1983 further Iranian attacks were mounted in the Mandali–Baghdad north-central sector. However, these were repelled by Iraqi mechanised and infantry divisions. By the end of 1983, an estimated one hundred and twenty thousand Iranians and sixty thousand Iraqis had been slaughtered.

From early 1983 Iran launched a series dawn operations that eventually numbered ten. During Operation Dawn-1, in February 1983, fifty thousand Iranian fighters attacked westward from Dezful and were confronted by fifty five thousand Iraqi fighters. An Iranian objective included cutting off the road from Basra to Baghdad to thwart their enemy. The Iraqis flew one hundred and fifty air sorties against the Iranians which included the bombing of Dezful, Ahvaz, and Khorramshahr. An Iraqi counter-attack was broken up by Iran's 92nd Armoured Division.

During April 1983 in Operation Dawn-2, the Iranians directed insurgency operations by proxy with their support for the Kurds in the North. Later, with Kurdish support, they attacked on the 23rd of July 1983 and captured the Iraqi town of Haj Omran and maintained it against an Iraqi poison gas counter-offensive. The Iranians attempted to further exploit activities in the north on the 30th of July, during Operation Dawn-3. Seeing an opportunity to sweep away Iraqi forces controlling the roads between the Iranian mountain border towns of Mehran, Dehloran and Elam.

Iraq then launched airstrikes, and equipped attack helicopters with chemical warheads. At the conclusion, seventeen thousand had been killed on both sides, with little gain for either country.

The focus of Operation Dawn-4 in September 1983 was the northern sector in Iranian Kurdistan. Three Iranian regular divisions amassed in Marivan and Sardasht in a move to threaten the Iraqi city of Suleimaniyah. To halt this activity, Iraq deployed Mi-8 attack helicopters equipped with chemical weapons and made one hundred and twenty sorties against the Iranian force, which stopped them fifteen kilometres into Iraqi territory. Five thousand Iranians and two and a half thousand Iraqis died. Iran gained one hundred and ten square kilometes of its territory back in the north, gained fifteen square kilometes of Iraqi land, and captured one thousand eight hundred Iraqi prisoners while Iraq abandoned large quantities of valuable weapons and war materiel in the field. Iraq responded to these losses by firing a series of SCUD-B missiles into the cities of Dezful, Masjid Soleiman, and Behbehan.

At the begining, the Iranians had outnumbered the Iraqis on the battlefield, but Iraq expanded its military draft, and by 1984, the armies were equal in size and, by 1986, Iraq had twice as many soldiers as Iran.

By 1988, Iraq boasted one million soldiers, making it's army the fourth largest in the world. Moreover, some of its equipment, such as tanks, outnumbered Iran's by at least five to one.

Following the Dawn Operations, Iran attempted to change tactics since up against increasing Iraqi defence, they could no longer rely on simple human wave attacks. Iranian offensives became more complex and involved extensive manoeuvre warfare using primarily light infantry and they launched frequent, and sometimes smaller offensives to slowly gain ground and deplete the Iraqis through attrition.

The Iranians hoped to drive Iraq into economic failure by squandering their money on weapons and war mobilization, deplete their population by bleeding them dry, and, in doing so, creating an anti-government insurgency.

The Iranian Army and Revolutionary Guards worked together better as their tactics improved and human wave attacks became less frequent, although still used. To neutralise the Iraqi advantage of heavy firepower, Iran began to focus on fighting in areas where the Iraqis could not use their heavy weaponry, such as marshes, valleys, and mountains, and frequently used infiltration tactics.

Iran commenced training troops in infiltration, patrolling, night-fighting, marsh warfare, and mountain warfare and also began training thousands of Revolutionary Guard commandos in amphibious warfare, since southern Iraq is marshy and has many wetland areas. Iran also learned to integrate foreign guerrilla units as part of their military operations. On the northern front, Iran began working a lot with the Peshmerga who were Kurdish guerrillas. Iranian military advisors organised the Kurds into raiding parties of a dozen guerrillas, which would attack Iraqi command posts, troop formations, infrastructure, including roads, supply lines and government buildings. The oil refineries of Kirkuk became a frequent target and were often hit by hand-made Peshmerga rockets.

By 1984, the Iranian ground forces were reorganised well enough for the Revolutionary Guard to start Operation Kheibar, which lasted for the duration of, from the 24th of February to the 19th of March. On the 15th of February 1984, the Iranians had begun launching attacks against the central section of the front, where the Second Iraqi Army Corps was deployed and there a quarter million Iraqis faced a quarter million Iranians. The goal of this new major offensive was the capture of the Basra to Baghdad Highway, cutting off Basra from Baghdad and setting the stage for an eventual attack upon the city. The Iraqi high command had assumed that the marshlands above Basra were natural barriers to attack, and had not reinforced them.

The marshes neutralised Iraqi advantage in armour and absorbed artillery rounds and bombs. The Iranians launched two preliminary attacks prior to the main offensive, Operation Dawn 5 and Dawn 6. Iranian troops crossed the river on motorboats in a surprise attack but only came within twenty four kilometres of the highway.

Operation Kheibar began on the 24th of February with Iranian infantrymen crossing the Hawizeh Marshes using motorboats and transport helicopters in an amphibious assault. They attacked the vital oil-producing Majnoon Island by landing troops via helicopters onto the islands and severing the communication lines between Amareh and Basra. They then continued the attack towards Qurna. By the 27th of February, they had captured the island, but suffered large helicopter losses to the Iraqis. On that day, a big fleet of Iranian helicopters transporting Pasdaran troops were intercepted by Iraqi combat aircraft including MiGs, Mirages and Sukhois. In what could be called an aerial slaughter, Iraqi jets shot down forty nine of the fifty Iranian helicopters. In places, combat took place in water over two metres deep where Iraqis had run live electrical cables through the water which electrocuted numerous Iranian troops and then they displayed their corpses on state television.

By the 29th of February, the Iranians had reached the outskirts of Qurna and were closing in on the Baghdad–Basra highway. They had come out of the marshes and returned to open terrain, where they were confronted by conventional Iraqi weapons, including artillery, tanks, air power, and mustard gas. Twelve hundred Iranian soldiers were killed in the counter-attack and the Iranians retreated back to the marshes.

The Battle of the Marshes saw an Iraqi defence that was relieved by their use of chemical weapons. They also largely relied on Mi-24 Hind to "hunt" the Iranian troops in the marshes, and at least twenty thousand Iranians were killed in the marsh battles. However, Iran used the marshes as a springboard for future attacks and infiltrations.

Four years into the war, the human cost to Iran had been one hundred and seventy thousand combat fatalities and three hundred and forty wounded. Iraqi combat fatalities were estimated at eighty thousand with one hundred and fifty thousand wounded.

Unable to launch successful ground attacks against Iran, Iraq used their now enlarged air force to carry out strategic bombing attacks against Iranian shipping and cities in trying to damage Iran's economy and morale. Saddam also wanted to provoke

Iran into doing something that would cause the superpowers to be directly involved in the conflict on the Iraqi side.

The aptly named "Tanker War" began when Iraq attacked the oil terminal and oil tankers at Kharg Island in early 1984 with the aim of, in attacking Iranian shipping, to provoke the Iranians to retaliate with extreme measures, such as closing the Strait of Hormuz to all maritime traffic. This would provoke American intervention since the United States had threatened several times to intervene if the Strait of Hormuz were closed. The result was though that the Iranians limited their retaliatory attacks to Iraqi shipping, thus leaving the strait open to general passage.

The Iraquis stated that all shipping going between Iranian ports in thePersian Gulf were risking attack. They used F-1 Mirage, Super Etendard, Mig-23, Su-20/22, and Super Frelon helicopters armed with Exocet anti-ship missiles as well as Soviet-made air-to-surface missiles to back up their threats. Iraq repeatedly bombed Iran's main oil export facility on Kharg Island, causing increasingly heavy damage. As an initial reaction to these attacks, Iran attacked a Kuwaiti tanker carrying Iraqi oil near Bahrain on the 13th of May 1984, and also a Saudi tanker in Saudi waters on the 16th of May.

Iraq had become increasingly landlocked during

the course of the war and had to rely on their Arab allies, primarily Kuwait, to transport their oil. Iran attacked tankers carrying Iraqi oil from Kuwait, later attacking tankers from any Persian Gulf state supporting Iraq. Attacks on ships of noncombatant nations in the Persian Gulf sharply increased thereafter, with both nations attacking oil tankers and merchant ships of neutral nations in an effort to deprive the enemy of trade. The Iranian attacks against Saudi shipping led to Saudi F-15s shooting down a pair of F-4 Phantom II fighters on the 5th of June 1984. The air and smaller boat attacks, however, did minimal damage to Persian Gulf economies and the Iranians moved their shipping port to Larak Island in the Strait of Hormuz.

The Iranian Navy imposed a naval blockade of Iraq in which they used British-built frigates to stop and inspect any shipping thought to be trading with Iraq. Some Iranian warships attacked tankers with missiles, while others used their radars to guide land-based anti-ship missiles. Iran also began premier use of its new Revolutionary Guard's navy, which used Boghammar speedboats fitted with rocket launchers and heavy machine guns. These launched surprise attacks against tankers and cause substantial damage. Iran also used F-4 Phantom II fighters and helicopters to launch Maverick missiles and unguided rockets at tankers.

An American Navy ship, Stark, was struck on the 17th of May 1987 by two Exocet anti-ship missiles fired from an Iraqi F-1 Mirage plane. The missiles had been fired at about the time the plane was given a routine radio warning by Stark. The frigate did not detect the missiles with radar, and warning was given by the lookout only moments before they struck. Both missiles hit the ship, and one exploded in crew quarters, killing thirty seven sailors and wounding twenty-one.

The British Insurers, Lloyd's of London, estimated that the Tanker War damaged five hundred and forty six commercial vessels and killed about four hundred and thirty civilian sailors. The largest portion of the attacks was directed by Iraq against vessels in Iranian waters, with the Iraqis launching three times as many attacks as the Iranians. But Iranian speedboat attacks on Kuwaiti shipping led Kuwait to formally petition foreign powers on the 1st of November 1986 to protect its shipping. The Soviet Union agreed to charter tankers starting in 1987, and the United States Navy offered to provide protection for foreign tankers reflagged and flying the U.S. flag starting the 7th of March 1987 in Operation Earnest Will. Neutral tankers shipping to Iran were not protected by Earnest Will, resulting in reduced foreign tanker traffic to Iran, since they risked Iraqi air attack resulting in the Iranian accusation of the United States helping Iraq.

At this time, Iraq's air force also commenced strategic bombing raids against Iranian cities. While Iraq had launched many attacks with aircraft and missiles against border cities from the beginning of the war and irregular raids on Iran's major cities, this became the first systematic strategic bombing that Iraq carried out during the war. These raids would earn the name "War of the Cities". In it, Iraq used Tu-22 Blinder and Tu-16 Badger strategic bombers to carry out long-range high-speed raids on Iranian cities, including Tehran. Fighter-bombers such as the MiG-25 Foxbat and Su-22 Fitter were used against smaller or shorter-range targets, as well as escorting the strategic bombers. Civilian and industrial targets were hit by the raids, and each successful raid inflicted more economic damage. In response, the Iranians used their F-4 Phantom planes to combat the Iraqis, eventually deploying F-14s too.

By 1986, Iran had also greatly expanded their air defence network to relieve the pressure on their air force. Later in the war, Iraqi raids primarily consisted of indiscriminate missile attacks whilst air attacks were used only on the fewer but more important targets. Beginning in 1987, Saddam also ordered several chemical attacks on civilian targets in Iran, including the town of Sardasht.

Iran launched several retaliatory air raids on Iraq, while primarily shelling border cities such as Basra and also bought some Scud missiles from Libya, launching them against Baghdad inflicting considerable damage upon the Iraquis. Ayatollah Khomeini urged Iranians on, declaring: It is our belief that Saddam wishes to return Islam to blasphemy and polytheism and if America becomes victorious and grants victory to Saddam, Islam will receive such a blow that it will not be able to raise its head for a long time. The issue is one of Islam versus blasphemy, and not of Iran versus Iraq.

For the remainder of 1986, and until the spring of 1988, the Iranian Air Force's efficiency in air defence increased, with weapons being repaired or replaced and new tactical methods being used.

The Iranians would loosely integrate their SAM Sites and interceptors to create "killing fields" in which dozens of Iraqi planes were lost. The Iraqi Air Force reacted by increasing the sophistication of its equipment, incorporating modern electronic countermeasure pods, decoys such as chaff and flare, and anti-radiation missiles.

Due to previous heavy plane losses, Iraq reduced their use of aerial attacks on Iranian cities and instead, they launched Scud missiles, which the Iranians had nothing stop. Iran responded to these attacks by using their own Scud missiles.

Adding to the problem of large foreign help to their enemy, The Iranians found their attacks were severely restricted by their shortages of weaponry, in particular, heavy weapons, having lost large amounts during the war. Iran, however, still managed to maintain a thousand tanks, often by capturing Iraqi ones, and additional artillery, many needing repairs to be fully operational. After some time, however, they did manage to procure spare parts from various sources, assisting them in restoring some weapons and they clandestinely imported further weapons. Iran also managed to get some advanced weapons, such as anti-tank TOW missiles, which worked better than rocket-propelled grenades.

On the night of the 10th of February 1986, the Iranians launched Operation Dawn 8. Thirty thousand troops in five Army divisions and men from the Revolutionary Guard and Basij advanced in a two-pronged offensive to capture the al-Faw peninsula in southern Iraq, the capture of which constituted a major goal for Iran. They began with a minor attack against Basra, which became halted by the Iraqis. Concurrently, an amphibious strike force landed at the bottom of the peninsula and the resistance, consisting of several thousand poorly trained soldiers of the Iraqi Popular Army, retreated or were defeated. The Iranian forces set up pontoon bridges crossing the Shatt al-Arab, allowing thirty thousand soldiers to cross quickly who drove north up the peninsula virtually unopposed and captured it after only twenty four hours there, after which they dug in and set up defences.

On the 12ᵗʰ of February 1986, the Iraqis began a counter-offensive to retake al-Faw, but this failed after one week of heavy fighting. On the 24th of February, Saddam sent one of his best commanders to begin a new offensive to recapture al-Faw. And then a fresh round of heavy fighting took place.

However, Iraqui counter-attacks again ended in failure, costing them many tanks and aircraft.The capture of al-Faw and the failure of Iraqi counter-offensives were seen as blows to the Ba'ath regime's prestige and this led Gulf countries to fear that Iran might win the war. The Kuwaitis felt menaced by Iranian troops being only sixteen kilometres away, and therefore increased its support of Iraq..

In March 1986, the Iranians attempted to follow up their success by trying to take Umm Qasr. This would have completely cut off Iraq from the Gulf and positioned Iranian troops on the border with Kuwait. The offensive, however, failed due to Iran's shortage of armour and weaponry. During this offensive, seventeen thousand Iraqi troops and thirty thousand Iranian troops became war casualties.

The First Battle of al-Faw wound up in March, but combat operations continued on the peninsula into 1988, with neither side being able to force out the other.

Shortly after the eventual Iranian capture of al-Faw, Saddam declared a new offensive against Iran, intended to drive deep into the country. The Iranian border city of Mehran, on the foot of the Zagros Mountains, was selected as the initial target. On the 15th to the 19th of May, Iraqi Army's Second Corps, supported by helicopter gunships, attacked and captured the city. The Iraquis then continued to attack, attempting to push deeper into Iran. Iraq's attack, however, was speedily deflected by Iranian AH-1 Cobra helicopters with TOW missiles, these destroying numerous Iraqi tanks and armoured vehicles.

The Iranians built up their forces on the heights surrounding Mehran and, on the 30th of June, using mountain warfare tactics they launched their attack. They had recaptured the city by the 3rd of July. Saddam ordered the Republican Guard to retake the city soon after but their attack was not effective.

Iraq sustained losses enough to allow the Iranians to further capture territory inside of Iraq. These outcomes reduced the Iraqi military enough to inhibit them from launching another major offensive for the following two years.

Through the eyes of international observers, Iran was prevailing in the war by the end of 1986. In the northern front, the Iranians began launching attacks toward the city of Suleimaniya with the help of Kurdish fighters, taking the Iraqis by surprise. They came within sixteen kilometres of the city before being stopped by chemical and other attacks.

Iran's army had also reached the Meimak Hills and were just one hundred and thirteen kilometres from the Iraqi capital, Baghdad. Iraq managed to limit Iran's offensives in the south, but was under intense pressure since the Iranians were gradually overwhelming them.

Iraq reacted by launching another 'war of the cities' and in one attack, Tehran's main oil refinery was hit. In another, Iraq damaged Iran's Assadabad satellite dish, disrupting Iranian overseas telephone and telex service for almost two weeks. Civilian areas were also hit, resulting in numerous casualties. Iraq continued to attack oil tankers by air and Iran responded by launching Scud missiles and air attacks at Iraqi targets.

In addition, Iraq continued to attack Kharg Island and the oil tankers and facilities. Iran, in an attempt to outmanoeuvre Irac, created a tanker shuttle service of twenty tankers to move oil from Kharg to Larak Island, escorted by Iranian fighter jets. Once moved to Larak, the oil would be transferred to ocean-going neutral tankers. They also rebuilt the oil terminals damaged by Iraqi air raids and they moved shipping to Larak Island and also carried out attacks on foreign tankers that carried Iraqi oil. The tanker war escalated dramatically, with attacks almost doubling in 1986 with the majority of them being carried out by Iraq.The escalating tanker war in the Gulf became an ever-increasing concern to foreign powers, especially to the United States.

In April 1986, Ayatollah Khomeini declared a fatwa stating that the war must be won by March 1987. The Iranians then increased recruitment efforts, obtaining six hundred and fifty thousand volunteers. Confident in its successes, Iran began planning their largest offensives of the war, which they named their "final offensives".

In the event of their recent defeats in al-Faw and Mehran, Iraq appeared to be losing the war and its generals, angered by Saddam's interference, threatened a full-scale mutiny against the Ba'ath Party unless they were allowed to carry out operations freely.

Saddam, in one of the few times of his career conceded to the demands of his generals. Up until this point, Iraqi strategy had been to ride out Iranian attacks. However, the defeat at al-Faw led Saddam to announce that all civilians had to take part in the war effort. The universities were closed and all of the male students were drafted into the military. Civilians were instructed to clear marshlands to prevent Iranian amphibious infiltrations and to help build fixed defences.

Saddam's government tried to integrate the Shias into the war effort by recruiting as many as they could to become part of the Ba'ath Party. In an attempt to counterbalance the religious fervour of the Iranians and gain support from the devout masses, the regime also began to promote religion and, on the surface,

Islamization, despite the fact that Iraq was run by a secular regime. Scenes of Saddam praying and making pilgrimages to shrines became common on state-run television. Iraqi morale had remained low throughout the war but the attack on al-Faw raised patriotic fervour since the Iraqis greatly feared invasion.

Saddam additionally recruited volunteers from other Arab countries into the Republican Guard, and received much technical support from foreign nations as well.

While Iraqi military power had got weaker due to recent battles, with foreign purchases and support, they were able to expand their military to even bigger levels by 1988.

At this time, Saddam also ordered the genocidal al-Anfal Campaign in an attempt to crush the Kurdish resistance, who were now allied with Iran. The result was the deaths of several hundred thousand Iraqi Kurds, and the destruction of villages, towns, and cities.

The Iraqi Republican Guard was expanded as a volunteer army and manned with Iraq's best generals. Loyalty to the state was no longer an absolute requisite for joining.

Iraq built its military massively, eventually possessing the 4th largest in the world, in order to overwhelm the Iranians through sheer size.

Iran, however, continued to attack as the Iraqis were planning their strikes. In 1987 the Iranians launched a series of major human wave offensives in both northern and southern Iraq. The Iraqis had elaborately fortified Basra with five defensive rings, exploiting natural waterways such as the Shatt-al-Arab and artificial ones, such as Fish Lake, a massive lake filled with mines, and the Jasim River, along with earth barriers, underwater barbed wire, electrodes and sensors. Behind each waterway and defensive line was radar-guided artillery, ground attack aircraft and helicopters, all capable of firing poison gas or using conventional munitions.

On the 25th of December 1986, Iran launched Operation Karbala-4. According to an Iraqi general, this was a diversionary attack. The Iranians also launched an amphibious assault against the Iraqi island of Umm al-Rassas in the Shatt-Al-Arab river, which was parallel to Khoramshahr. They then set up a pontoon bridge and continued the attack, eventually capturing the island but failing to advance further. The Iranians sustained sixty thousand casualties, while the Iraqis had only nine and a half thousand.

When Operation Karbala 5, the main Iranian

attack, began, many Iraqi troops were on leave. This offensive, also known as the Siege of Basra, was an operation carried out by Iran in an effort to capture the Iraqi port city in early 1987. This battle, with its extensive casualties, was the biggest battle of the war and proved to be the beginning of the end of the Iran–Iraq War.

While Iranian forces crossed the border and captured the eastern section of Basra, the operation ended in a stalemate.

At the same time as Operation Karbala 5, Iran also launched Operation Karbala-6 against the Iraqis in Qasr-e Shirin in central Iran to prevent the Iraqis from quickly bringing units down to defend against the Karbala-5 attack. This attack was carried out by Basij infantry and the Revolutionary Guard's 31st Ashura and the Army's 77th Khorasan armoured divisions. The Basij attacked the Iraqi lines, forcing the Iraqi infantry to retreat. An Iraqi armoured counter-attack surrounded the Basij in a pincer movement, but the Iranian tank divisions attacked, breaking the encirclement. The Iranian attack was finally stopped by mass Iraqi chemical weapons attacks. The results of Operation Karbala-5 turned out to be a severe blow to both Iran's military and its morale.

To foreign observers, it had appeared that Iran was continuing to strengthen. By 1988, it had become self-sufficient in many areas, such as anti-tank TOW missiles, Scud ballistic missiles, Silkworm anti-ship missiles, Oghab tactical rockets, and producing spare parts for their weaponry. Iran had also improved its air defenses with smuggled surface to air missiles and was even producing UAV's and the Pilatus PC-7 propeller aircraft for observation. The Iranians also doubled their stocks of artillery, and became self-sufficient in the manufacture of ammunition and small arms.

While it was not obvious to foreign observers, the Iranian public had become increasingly war-weary and disillusioned with the fighting, and relatively few volunteers had joined the fighting in the years 1987 and 1988. Because the Iranian war effort depended on popular mobilization, their military strength actually declined, and Iran was unable to launch any major offensives after Karbala-5. As a result, for the first time since 1982, the momentum of the fighting shifted towards the regular army and since the regular army was conscription based, it made the war ever less popular.

Many ordinary Iranians began to try to escape the conflict and, as early as May 1985, anti-war demonstrations took place in seventy-four cities throughout Iran. These, however, were crushed by the regime, resulting in some protesters being shot and killed. But by 1987, draft-dodging had become a serious problem and the Revolutionary Guards and police set up roadblocks throughout cities to capture those who tried to evade conscription.

The leadership acknowledged that the war was a stalemate, and began to plan accordingly. No more "final offensives" were planned and the head of the Supreme Defence Council announced during a news conference that the end of human wave attacks had come. Sanctions, declining oil prices, and Iraqi attacks on Iranian oil facilities and shipping took a heavy toll on the Iranian economy.

Iranian oil and non-oil exports fell by 55%, inflation reached 50% by 1987, and unemployment skyrocketed. At the same time, Iraq was experiencing crushing debt and shortages of workers, encouraging its leadership to try to end the war quickly.

By the end of 1987, Iraq possessed 5,550 tanks which outnumbered the Iranians six to one and 900 fighter aircraft outnumbering the Iranians ten to one. After Operation Karbala-5, Iraq only had one hundred qualified fighter pilots remaining; therefore, Iraq began to invest in recruiting foreign pilots from countries such as Belgium, South Africa, Pakistan, East Germany and the Soviet Union. They replenished their manpower by integrating volunteers from other Arab countries into their army. Iraq also became self-sufficient in chemical weapons and some conventional ones and received much equipment from overseas. Foreign support helped Iraq bypass its economic troubles and massive debt to continue the war and increase the size of its military.

While the southern and central fronts were at a stalemate, Iran began to focus on carrying out offensives in northern Iraq with the help of the Peshmerga, using a combination of semi-guerrilla and infiltration tactics in the Kurdish mountains. During Operation Karbala-9 in early April, Iran captured territory near Suleimaniya, provoking a severe poison gas counterattack. During Operation Karbala-10, Iran attacked near the same area, capturing more territory. During Operation Nasr-4, the Iranians surrounded the city of Suleimaniya and, with the help of the Peshmerga, infiltrated over 140 km into Iraq andthreatened to capture the oil-rich city of Kirkuk and other northern oilfields. Nasr-4 was considered to be Iran's most successful individual operation of the war but Iranian forces were unable to consolidate their gains and continue their advance.

On the 20th of July, the UN Security Council passed the U.S.-sponsored Resolution 598, which called for an end to the fighting and a return to pre-war boundaries. This resolution was noted by Iran for being the first resolution to call for a return to the pre-war borders.

With a stalemate on land, the air-to-tanker war began increasingly to play an major role in the conflict. The Iranian air force had become diminished, with only twenty F-4 Phantoms, twenty F-5 Tigers, and fifteen F-14 Tomcats in operation. The Iranian

Air Force was unable to lead an outright onslaught against Iraq. The Iraqi Air Force, however, had originally lacked modern equipment and experienced pilots, but after pleas from Iraqi military leaders, Saddam decreased his political influence on everyday operations, leaving the fighting to the combatants. The Soviets began delivering more advanced aircraft and weapons to Iraq, while the French improved training for flight crews and technical personnel and continually introduced new methods for countering Iranian weapons and tactics. However, Iranian ground air defense still shot down many Iraqi aircraft.

The principle Iraqi air effort had changed to the destruction of Iran's war-fighting capability, principally Gulf oil fields, tankers, and Kharg Island. Beginning in late 1986, the Iraqi Air Force began a broad campaign against the Iranian economic infrastructure and by late 1987, they could depend on direct American support for carrying out long-range operations against Iranian infrastructural targets and oil installations deep into the Arabian Gulf. In the colossal Iraqi air strike against Kharg Island, perpetrated on the 18th of March 1988, the Iraqis destroyed two super-tankers but lost five aircraft to Iranian F-14 Tomcats. The U.S. Navy now became more involved in the fight in the Arabian Gulf. They launched Operations Earnest Will and Prime Chance against the Iranians.

The attacks on oil tankers continued. Both Iran and Iraq carried out frequent attacks during the first four months of 1988. In 1987, Kuwait asked to reflag its tankers to the U.S. flag. They did so in March, and the U.S. Navy began Operation Earnest Will to escort the tankers. The result of Earnest Will would be that, while oil tankers shipping Iraqi/Kuwaiti oil were protected, Iranian tankers and neutral tankers shipping to Iran would be unprotected, resulting in both losses for Iran and the undermining of its trade with foreign countries, damaging Iran's economy further. The United States began to escort the reflagged tankers, but one was damaged by a mine while under escort. While being a public-relations victory for Iran, the United States increased its reflagging efforts. While Iran mined the Arbian Gulf, their speedboat attacks were reduced, primarily attacking unflagged tankers in the area.

During that November and December, the Iraqi air force launched a bid to destroy all Iranian airbases in Khuzestan and the remaining Iranian air force. Iran managed to shoot down thirty Iraqi fighters with fighter jets, anti-aircraft guns, and missiles, enabling the Iranian air force to survive to the end of the war.

On the 28th of June, Iraqi fighter bombers had attacked the Iranian town of Sardasht near the border, using chemical mustard gas bombs. Many Iranian towns had been bombed before, and troops attacked with gas, but this was the first time that the Iraqis had made a chemical attack on a civilian area. Approximately a quarter of the twenty thousand population was burned and stricken, and one hundred and thirteen killed immediately. Many more died or suffered health effects over ensuing decades.

By 1988, with massive equipment imports Iraq was ready to launch major new offensives against Iran. In February 1988, Saddam launched the fifth and most deadly war of the cities. Over the ensuing two months, Iraq launched over two hundred al-Hussein missiles at thirty seven Iranian cities. Saddam also threatened to use chemical weapons in his missiles which caused a third of Tehran's population to flee the city. Iran did retaliate and launched over a hundred missiles against Iraq in 1988 including the shelling of Basra. These events were called the "Scud Duel" by the international media.

In March 1988, the Iranians carried out Operation Dawn 10, Operation Beit ol-Moqaddas 2, and Operation Zafar 7 in Iraqi Kurdistan with the aim of capturing the Darbandikhan Dam and the power plant at Lake Dukan, which supplied Iraq with much of its electricity and water, as well as the city of Suleimaniya. The Iranians had hoped that the capture of these areas would bring more favourable terms to any ceasefire agreement. Iranian airborne commandos landed behind the Iraqi lines and Iranian helicopters hit Iraqi tanks with TOW missiles. The Iraqis were taken by surprise, and Iranian F-5E Tiger fighter jets were able to damage the Kirkuk oil refinery.

The Iranians then used infiltration tactics in the Kurdish mountains, captured the town of Halabja and began to fan out across the province. Though they advanced to within sight of Dukan and captured over one thousand square kilometres and four thousand Iraqi troops, their offensive failed when the Iraqis launched the deadliest chemical weapons attacks of the war. They unleashed a chemical cloud over the Iranians. The Iraqi special forces then stopped the remains of the Iranian force. In revenge for Kurdish collaboration with the Iranians, Iraq then launched a massive poison gas attack against Kurdish civilians in Halabja killing thousands of civilians.

On the 17th of April 1988, Iraq launched a surprise attack against the fifteen thousand Basij troops on the al-Faw peninsula. The attack was preceded by Iraqi diversionary attacks in northern Iraq, with a massive artillery and air barrage of Iranian front lines. Key points including supply lines, command posts, and ammunition depots, were hit by a storm of mustard and nerve gases, and also by conventional explosives. Helicopters landed Iraqi commandos behind Iranian lines on al-Faw while the main Iraqi force made a head-on assault. Within two days the Iranian forces were either killed or had fled from the al-Faw Peninsula.The heavy and expert use of chemical weapons was the decisive factor in the Iraqi victory.

The same day as Iraq's attack on al-Faw peninsula, the United States Navy launched Operation Praying Mantis in retaliation against Iran for damaging a warship with a mine. The defeats at al-Faw and in the Arabian Gulf helped persuade the Iranian leadership to consider quitting the war, exacerbated by the possibility of needing to fight with the Americans.

Due in part to the losses, Khomeini appointed the cleric Hashemi Rafsanjani to the position of Supreme Commander of the Armed Forces. Rafsanjani ordered a final counter-attack into Iraq, which was launched the 13th of June 1988. The Iranians infiltrated through the Iraqi trenches and moved ten kilometres into Iraq. After three days of fighting, the decimated Iranians were driven back to their original positions again as the Iraqis launched nearly a thousand aircraft sorties.

On the 18th of June 1988, Iraq launched Operation Forty Stars in conjunction with the Mujahideen-e-Khalq around Mehran. With five hundred and thirty aircraft sorties and heavy use of nerve gas, they smashed the Iranian forces there, killing three and a half thousand and almost destroying a Revolutionary Guard division. Mehran was captured once again and occupied by the Mujahideen. Iraq also launched air raids on Iranian population centres and economic targets, igniting numerous oil installations.

On the 25th of May 1988, Iraq launched of one of the biggest artillery barrages in history, as well as use of chemical weapons. The Iraqis also used tanks to bypass Iranian field fortifications and expelled the Iranians from the border town of Shalamcheh after a battle of less than ten hours.

On the 25th of June 1988, Iraq launched the second of their Tawakal ala Allah operations against the Iranians on Majnoon Island. Iraqi commandos used amphibious craft to block the Iranian rear, then used hundreds of tanks with massed conventional and chemical artillery barrages to recapture the island after eight hours of combat. The majority of the Iranian defenders were killed during the quick assault and the final two Tawakal ala Allah operations took place near al-Amarah and Khaneqan. By the 12th of July 1988 the Iraqis had captured the city of Dehloran, thirty kilometres inside Iran, and captured two and a half thousand troops and along with abundant armour and material. This took four days to transport to Iraq. The Iranian losses included more than half of the one thousand remaining Iranian tanks, plus armoured vehicles, self-propelled artillery, towed artillery pieces, and anti-aircraft guns.

On the 2nd of July 1988, Iran belatedly set up a joint central command which unified the Revolutionary Guard, Army, and Kurdish rebels, and dispelled the rivalry between the Army and the Revolutionary Guard.

Saddam sent a warning to Khomeini in mid-1988, threatening to launch a new and powerful full-scale invasion and attack Iranian cities with weapons of mass destruction. Shortly afterwards, Iraqi aircraft bombed the Iranian town of Oshnavieh with poison gas, immediately killing and wounding over two thousand civilians.

The lives of the civilian population of Iran were becoming extremely disrupted, with a third of the urban population evacuating major cities in fear of an apparantly imminent chemical war. Meanwhile, Iraqi explosive bombs and missiles frequently hit towns and cities and destroyed vital civilian and military infrastructure besides increasing the death toll. Iran replied with missile and air attacks, but could not stop the Iraqis.

On the 14th of July, under threat of a fresh and even more powerful Iraqi invasion, Commander-in-Chief Rafsanjani ordered his forces to retreat from Haj Omran. The Iranians did not publicly describe this as a retreat, but called it a temporary withdrawal. By July 1988, Iran's army inside of Iraq had mostly disintegrated. However, Iraq had suffered heavy losses too and the battles were severely costly.

In July 1988, Iraqi aircraft dropped bombs on the

Iranian Kurdish village of Zardan. Dozens of villages, including Sardasht, as well as some larger towns, including Marivan, Baneh and Saqqez, were once again attacked with poison gas, causing even heavier civilian casualties.

At this point, members of the Iranian leadership, led by Rafsanjani, persuaded Khomeini to accept a ceasefire. On the 20th of July 1988, Iran accepted Resolution 598, showing its willingness to accept a ceasefire.

The last notable combat actions of the war took place on the 3rd of August 1988, in the Persian Gulf when the Iranian navy fired on a freighter and Iraq launched chemical attacks on Iranian civilians, killing an unknown number of them and wounding over two thousand. Resolution 598 became effective on the 8th of August 1988, ending all combat operations between the two countries. By the 20th of August 1988, peace with Iran was restored. UN peacekeepers belonging to the United Nations Iran–Iraq Military Observer Group mission took the field, remaining on the Iran–Iraq border until 1991.

THE SEPTEMBER 11 ATTACKS

The attacks of the eleventh of September 2001, often referred to as 9/11, were four coordinated suicide terrorist attacks perpetrated by the Islamist extremist network al-Qaeda against the United States of America. That morning, nineteen terrorists hijacked four commercial airliners scheduled to travel from the East Coast of America to California on the West Coast. The hijackers crashed the first two planes into the Twin Towers of the World Trade Centre in New York City, and the third into the Pentagon, the headquarters of the United States military, in Arlington County, Virginia near Washington, D.C. The fourth plane was s intended to hit a federal government building in Washington D.C. but crashed into a field after a revolt by passengers. The attacks brought the deaths of almost three thousand people and ignited a global war on terror.

The initial impact was that of American Airlines Flight 11 when it was crashed into the North Tower of the World Trade Center complex in Lower Manhattan at 8:46 a.m. that day. Just seventeen minutes later the World Trade Centre's South Tower was hit by United Airlines Flight 175. The two one-hundred-and-ten story skyscrapers collapsed within one hour and three quarters of the initial impact, which brought about the destruction of the remaining five structures in the World Trade Centre complex. A third plane, American Airlines Flight 77, was crashed into the Pentagon at 9.37 a.m., causing it to partially collapse. The fourth and final flight, United Airlines Flight 93, flew in the direction of Washington, D.C. Hearing of the previous attacks, some of the passengers attempted to gain control of the aircraft, but the hijackers crashed the plane into a field in Stonycreek Township, Pennsylvania, near Shanksville at 10:03 a.m., killing everyone on board.

Within a few hours of the attacks, the CIA were convinced that the Islamic terrorist organisation, al-Qaeda was responsible. The United States formally responded by launching its war on terror, leading to an invasion of Afghanistan to depose the Taliban, an Afghani Islamic organisation which they believed was sheltering Osama bin Laden, al-Queda's leader. America's invocation of Article 5 of the North Atlantic Treaty called upon allies to help fight al-Qaeda.

As U.S. and NATO ground forces swept through Afghanistan, Osama bin Laden fled to the White Mountains, where he narrowly avoided capture by the U.S. led forces. It was only in 2004 that Osama bin-Laden formally claimed responsibility for the attacks with Al-Qaeda citing motivations included the U.S.A's support of Israel, the presence of U.S. troops in Saudi Arabia, and sanctions against Iraq. After evading capture for almost ten years, Osama bin Laden was killed by the U.S. military on the 2nd of May, 2011. However, U.S. and NATO troops remained in Afghanistan until 2021.

The 9/11 attacks resulted in 2,977 non-hijacker fatalities, an indeterminate number of injuries, and substantial long-term health consequences, in addition to at least ten billion dollars in infrastructure and property damage. It remains the most deadly terrorist attack in history. The destruction of the World Trade Center and its environs seriously harmed the New York City economy and induced global market shocks. Many other countries strengthened anti-terrorism legislation and expanded their powers of law enforcement and intelligence agencies. Clean up of the World Trade Centre site (colloquially "Ground Zero") took eight months and was completed in May 2002, while the Pentagon was repaired within a year. After delays in the design of a replacement complex, the One World Trade Centre began construction in November 2006 and opened in November 2014. Memorials to the attacks include the National September 11 Memorial & Museum in New York City, the Pentagon Memorial in Arlington County, Virginia, and the Flight 93 National Memorial at the Pennsylvania crash site.

Shortly before the U.S. presidential election in 2004, Osama bin Laden used a taped statement to publicly acknowledge al-Qaeda's involvement in the attacks on the United States and said he had personally directed his followers to attack the World Trade Centre and the Pentagon. The U.S. never formally indicted bin Laden for the September 11 attacks, but he was on the FBI's Most Wanted List for the bombings of the U.S. Embassies in Dar es Salaam, Tanzania, and Nairobi, Kenya. Following a ten-year manhunt, U.S. President Barack Obama announced that Osama bin Laden had been killed by American special forces in a compound in Abbottabad, Pakistan, on the first of May, 2011.

Osama Bin Laden had interpreted Muhammad as having banned the "permanent presence of infidels in Arabia." In 1998, al-Qaeda had written: "for over seven years the United States has been occupying the lands of Islam in the holiest of places, the Arabian Peninsula, plundering its riches, dictating to its rulers, humiliating its people."

THE 2004 MADRID TRAIN BOMBINGS

The train bombings in Madrid, Spain, in 2004 were a series of coordinated, almost simultaneous bombings against the Cercanías commuter train system of Madrid, on the morning of the 11th of March that year, three days before Spain's general elections. The explosions killed one hundred and ninety three people and injured approximately two thousands. The official investigation by the Spanish judiciary declared that the attacks were directed by al-Qaeda, allegedly as a retaliation against Spain's involvement in the 2003 US-led invasion of Iraq.

On the 14th of March 2004, Abu Dujana al-Afghani, a purported spokesman for al-Qaeda in Europe, appeared in a videotape claiming responsibility for the attacks.

The Spanish judiciary stated that a loose group of Moroccan, Syrian, and Algerian Muslims and two Guardia Civil and Spanish police informants were suspected of having carried out the attacks. On the 11th of April 2006, Judge Juan del Olmo charged twenty nine suspects for their involvement in the train bombings. In August 2007, al-Qaeda claimed to be "proud" about the Madrid 2004 bombings.

On the 25th of March 2005, prosecutor Olga Sánchez asserted that the bombings happened nine hundred and eleven days, which was exactly two and a half years, after the 11th of September attacks due to the "highly symbolic and kabbalistic charge for local Al-Qaida groups" of choosing that day. Because 2004 was a leap year, 912 days had elapsed between the 11th of September 2001 and the 11th of March 2004.

THE 2005 LONDON BOMBINGS

These bombings, sometimes called 7/7, were a sequence of four coordinated suicide bomb attacks carried out by Islamic terrorists that targeted commuters travelling on London's public transport system that 7th of July during the busiest time of the morning. Firstly, three terrorists separately detonated purpose-made bombs in quick succession on board London Underground trains across the city. Later, a fourth terrorist detonated another bomb on a double-decker bus in Tavistock Square, London WC1.

The train bombings happened on the Circle line near Aldgate EC3, at Edgware Road,W2 and on the Piccadilly Line near Russell Square, WC1. The explosions were caused by improvised explosive devices made from triacetone triperoxide, packed into backpacks.

In addition to the bombers, fifty two UK residents spread across eighteen different nationalities were killed and more than seven hundred were injured in the attacks.

It was almost one hour after the train attacks that the fourth bomb exploded on the top deck of a number

30 double-decker bus as it was travelling its route from Marble Arch to Hackney Wick. The bus had left Marble Arch at 9 a.m. and had arrived at Euston bus station at 9:35 a.m., where crowds of people had been evacuated from the Underground railway and were boarding buses as an alternative.

The explosion at 9:47 a.m. in Tavistock Square blew off the roof and destroyed the rear portion of the bus and it took place near BMA House, the headquarters of the British Medical Association, on Upper Woburn Place where a number of doctors and medical staff being nearby, were able to offer immediate emergency medical assistance.

The extent of the damage caused to the victims' bodies resulted in a lengthy delay in announcing the death toll from the bombing while the police determined how many bodies were at the scene and if or not the bomber's body was amongst them.

The fifty-two victims were of diverse backgrounds and all were UK residents, thirty two victims being British, while one victim came from Afghanistan, one from France, one from Ghana, one from Grenada, one from India, one from Iran, one from Israel, one from Italy, one from Kenya, one from Mauritius, one from New Zealand, one from Nigeria, one from Romania, one from Sri Lanka one from Turkey, three from Poland and one was a Vietnamese born Australian and one held dual American-Vietnamese citizenship.

The four suicide bombers were later identified as: Mohammad Sidique Khan, aged 30. He lived in Beeston, Leeds, with his wife and young child, where he worked as a learning mentor at a primary school. He detonated his bomb on the number 216 train, killing seven people, including himself. Shehzad Tanweer, aged 22 lived in Leeds with his mother and father, working in a fish and chip shop. He detonated his bomb on the number 204 train. Killing seven other people. Germaine Lindsay, aged nineteen lived in Aylesbury, Buckinghamshire with his pregnant wife and young son. He detonated his device on the number 311 train killing twenty-seven people, including himself. Hasib Hussain, aged 18, lived in Leeds with his brother and sister-in-law. He detonated his bomb on the bus at Tavistock Square, killing fourteen people, including himself.

Three of the bombers were British-born sons of Pakistani immigrants; Germaine Lindsay was an Islamic convert born in Jamaica.

On the day of the bombings, the four had travelled to Luton, in Bedfordshire, by car, and then to London by train where they were filmed on CCTV arriving at King's Cross station at about 8:30 a.m.

Two of the bombers made videotapes describing their reasons for becoming what they called "soldiers".Mohammad Khan's tape stated: "I and thousands like me are forsaking everything for what we believe. Our drive and motivation doesn't come from tangible commodities that this world has to offer. Our religion is Islam, obedience to the one true God and following the footsteps of the final prophet messenger. Your democratically-elected governments continuously perpetuate atrocities against my people all over the world and your support of them makes you directly responsible, just as I am directly responsible for protecting and avenging my Muslim brothers and sisters. Until we feel security you will be our targets and until you stop the bombing, gassing, imprisonment and torture of my people, we will not stop this fight. We are at war and I am a soldier

EPILOGUE

As this book was being edited, another war between religions has sparked into being, or more accurately, has been rekindled. Since the start of the 1948 Arab Israeli war, many thousands of civilians and soldiers have lost their lives.

On the 7th of October 2023, an armed conflict broke out between Israel and Hamas-led Palestinian militants from the Gaza Strip after the Palestinian militant groups launched a barrage of rockets against Israel, while around 3,000 militants breached the Gaza–Israel barrier attacking Israeli military bases and civilians in more than a dozen massacres, including one at a music festival. Over two hundred Israeli civilians and soldiers, as well as some foreign nationals, were taken captive to the Gaza Strip. Hamas representatives said its attack was in response to the blockade on Gaza, continued settlements, Israeli settler violence, and restrictions on movement between Israel and Gaza.

Israel's declaration of a state of war the following day marked the start of the most significant military escalation in the region since the Yom Kippur War;

its lengthy aerial bombardment of Gaza dropped 6,000 bombs in the first six days of the conflict. The airstrikes were coordinated with a total blockade of the Gaza strip in addition to cutting off water, fuel, food and electricity. Israel urged one-point-one million Palestinians to evacuate northern Gaza, while Hamas called on residents to stay in their homes.

Widespread civilian deaths led to both Israel and Hamas being accused of war crimes. The United Nations reported that around one-point-five million Palestinians, over seventy percent of Gaza's population, and also over two thousand Israelis have been internally displaced. There became acute shortages of drinking water, food and fuel in Gaza. The Gazan health system was failing; more than half of all hospitals being out of service due to shortages of fuel and power, and medical surgeries like C-sections and amputations were being performed without anesthetic due to shortages of medical supplies. The war has led to widespread global protests that have focused on a variety of issues including demands for a ceasefire, and the release of hostages. Pro-Palestinian anti-war protests in particular have been described as the largest since those against the Iraq War in 2003.